FRACTALS

The Invisible World of Fractals
Made Visible Through Theater and Dance

KIMBERLEY CETRON

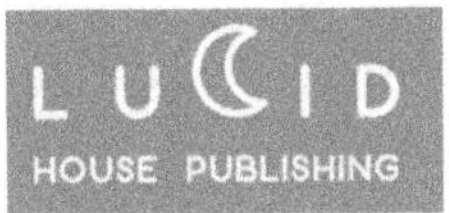

Published in Atlanta, Georgia, United States of America by Lucid House Publishing, LLC
www.LucidHousePublishing.com

© 2021 by Kimberley Cetron
First Edition. All rights reserved. Printed in the United States.
This title is also available as an e-book via Lucid House Publishing, LLC
Cover and Design Director: Troy King
Author photo: Julie Napear Photography
Citations begin on page 151.
All credited photography in this book is used with permission.

Library of Congress Cataloging-in-Publication Data
Cetron, Kimberley, 1963-
Fractals/ the invisible world of fractals made visible through theater and dance
Kimberley Cetron–1st U.S. ed.
ISBN: 978-1-950495-13-9
Library of Congress Control Number: 2021934456
1. fractals 2. theater-dance collaborations 3. interdisciplinary education 4. STEAM
5. Total Theatre Artist 6. poetry 7. spoken word

EDU057000
PER003000
PER011000

Discounts on bulk sales for classroom use or other group sales may be available by contacting the publisher at info@LucidHousePublishing.com.

Praise for *FRACTALS*

"The ideas, concepts, and principles explored in *FRACTALS* deliver fresh insight for practitioners of diverse forms of art. It offers truth in the matter – that education truly involves collaboration. Our histories lead us to new pathways and new ways of thinking: and within that, it is our nature to share and build new knowledge together."

—Autumn Eckman
Dancer, Choreographer, and Assistant Professor of
Dance, University of Arizona

*   *   *

"Kimberley Cetron's deep dive into the connective relationships between dramatic impulsive movement text and choreography is a gold mine. It offers endless possibilities for artistic educational conversation."

—Tomé Cousin
Dancer, Choreographer, Director, and
Associate Professor of Dance, Carnegie Mellon University

*   *   *

"As a playwright, people often ask me what I do when I need inspiration. I tell them, 'I watch modern dance.' Now, thanks to Dr. Kimberley Cetron's lucid and vibrant book *FRACTALS*, I understand that dance helps me see and respond to the mathematical chaos and inherent order in the natural world. I now understand that I am responding to the geometric beauty and mystery of fractals.

By introducing us to her illuminating work, methodology, and research in creating the celebrated theater-dance piece *Fractals*, Dr. Cetron introduces artists to a world of possibility and inspiration by helping us see what was visible already: that everything is unique, and yet part of a pattern. For artists looking to deepen their craft, expand their vision, and ground the thematic nature of their art the answer is simple: open your eyes and listen. Unpredictability and rhythm work in tandem in the natural world and should be part of your creative process as well. As Cetron points out, van Gogh captured patterns in turbulence rather than the darkness of the night. Both an inspiring and practical read about putting theory into practice."

—Karen Zacarías
Playwright, founder of Young Playwrights' Theater

*   *   *

"As a performer, director, and choreographer, I was intrigued by the ideas brought forth in *FRACTALS*. Any path to honest creation in the journey of actors who dance and dancers who act is worth the time spent reading and understanding the information presented. *FRACTALS* opened and expanded my mind, and that is what I believe will propel theatre forward.

—Gregory Butler
Director, Choreographer, Writer, Actor, Singer, Dancer

*   *   *

"I was a triple threat when I was performing full time, and as a director I know how important it is to hire people who can do it all. Now that I teach at the college level, I push young performers to be triple threats and more. In my experience, it was always the 'something extra' that helped me to get work, so I push for this in developing young artists. *FRACTALS* is an important source of information, for actors and for teachers. In today's market, you have to be able to work outside your comfort zone and explore all aspects of your craft. This book offers a glimpse into the worlds of people who have."

—John Vincent Leggio
Director, Choreographer, Broadway Veteran; Teacher at Steps On Broadway and Montclair State University

"The real voyage of discovery consists not in seeking new landscapes, but in having new eyes."

— Marcel Proust

CONTENTS

PREFACE

The first question people ask about this book is: *What are fractals?* You may be asking that yourself. There is not a simple answer. At their most essential, fractals are patterns. In order to be fractal, they must have self-similarity in shape, infinite reiteration, and fractal dimension (between 3D and 4D). Fractal patterns occur in nature, in anatomy, in cloud formations, in mountain ranges, all around us.

Most of us learned Euclidian geometry in school, constructed shapes, the geometry of the man-made world. It was not until the 1970s that Benoit Mandelbrot discovered a geometry that could apply to the natural world instead. The easiest example to consider is a tree. It establishes a pattern with its first branches that replicates as far as its branches go. The same pattern replicates from the largest branches to the smallest twigs. The pattern would continue into infinity if the tree grew that far. Clusters of trees establish a pattern that replicates throughout the forest. Often the fruit that grows on them can be cut in half to reveal fractal patterns. The cones that others form are fractals. There is a great deal more information in this book about what they are and where they are. They are not too complicated for anyone to understand, on some level. I confess to a limited mathematical grasp of what they are. I invite you to start somewhere and build on your knowledge.

You may not want to start at the beginning of this book. You may want to begin in the annotated section of Chapter 3 and build a

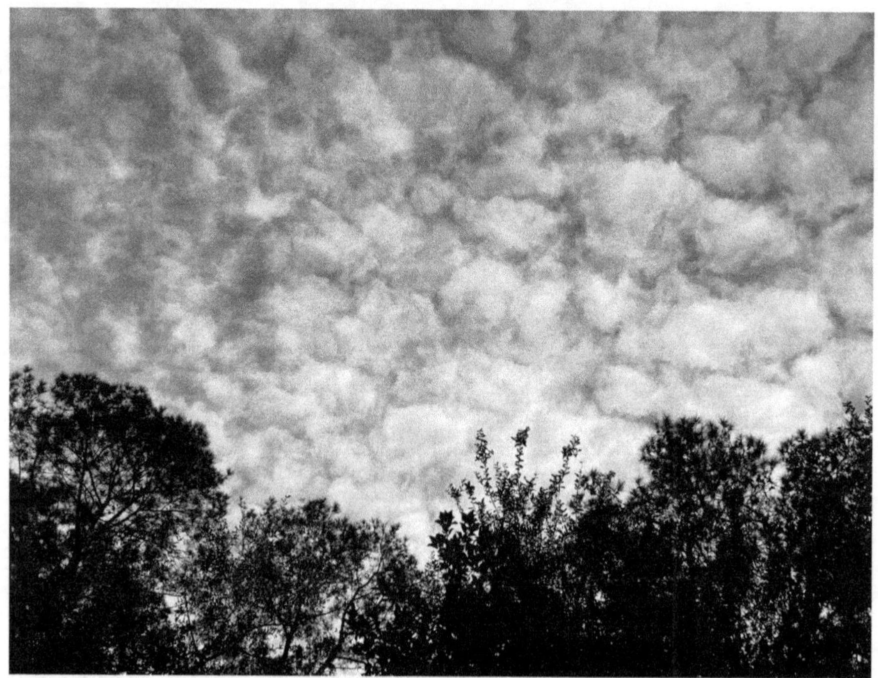

Fractal patterns in clouds and trees
Photo credit: LeeAnn Kole Photography

working knowledge of fractals first. Use this book in a way that best serves you.

You may be coming to this book without a working knowledge of theater. There is very little terminology that will prove confusing, but in case it does, those terms appear at the end of this preface.

You may be coming to the book wanting to know how to use theater and dance to teach fractals, or to teach another academic subject through performance art. In that case, the opening chapters may interest you, but you probably want to learn about fractals from the annotated text in Chapter 3 and focus on the applications in Chapter 5.

You may be a writer, or a writing teacher, using this as an example of ways to use multiple genres to write for understanding of a complex subject – or ways to write across genres in order to communicate complexity clearly. Those ideas are modeled throughout the book but are a focus in Chapters 3 and 5.

You may be in the theater-dance communities, or an arts educator, in which case you will most likely benefit from the whole work or want to focus on understanding fractals first and then seeking ways to create your own productions based on the material in Chapter 5. Chapters 1-4 describe the way we did it. You will make discoveries of your own.

In 2016, Meredith Barnes (dancer, choreographer, dance educator) called me to discuss producing a show about fractals. At the time it was an idea and a couple of completed dances. She wanted to be sure that the result would be a theater-dance collaboration and not a dance concert. The July 2016 festival production was successful and led us to want more – an opportunity to build on the production we created, and to provide a map so that others would create similar collaborations. This was our purpose in publishing our script and our process.

In the time it has taken to publish this, new ideas, new information, and new productions keep appearing. We will endeavor to keep this information updated via the electronic version of the book.

Please reach out with ideas, with questions, and with contributions to this body of knowledge, for the good of us all. Find us on Facebook at Fractals (user name @FractalsByCetron).

REGARDING CITATIONS

As a reader of non-fiction, I enjoy works that present information without interruption for citations or footnotes. I feel just as strongly about respect for intellectual property. That being said, I cite all the works that informed my writing of both the play *Fractals* and this book chapter-by-chapter in the *Notes* that appear at the end of this work.

THEATER TERMINOLOGY

Triple-threat performer: A performer skilled in acting, singing, and dance. Recent theater history has spawned the need for performers who can also play a musical instrument.

Load-in and load-out: Bringing the set, lighting, sound, props, and costumes into the performance venue (load-in) and removing them after the performance or the run of the show (load-out, or strike).

Tech – Technical rehearsal: A rehearsal when lighting and sound are added to the performance. These are typically start-and-stop rehearsals where the lighting and sound are adjusted and finalized. Sometimes the entire production is rehearsed, and sometimes the performers skip from one (lighting and sound) cue to the next.

Swings: Performers who prepare to cover any role or roles in the show when another performer is absent.

INTRODUCTION

Everything has changed.

The worlds of theater and dance, the world of education, even the natural world which provides the foundation of fractals as we understand them – these have all changed.

In the nascent stages of this production, and of this book, we could not have imagined the world as it is today: the universality of staying home; of shuttered businesses and schools; of conducting our lives via web conferencing. We lack the vantage point to envision what the world will be like when we return to it. All we know is that it will not be the same. We have evolved. Things cannot go back to the way they were, back to normal. There is no normal to which we can return.

What hasn't changed is our desire to connect, to express, to communicate. It is astonishing to witness, in just a few months' time, the innovations in the ways we educate, inform, create, and collaborate. The natural world is experiencing a rebirth we could not have imagined. Trees emerge in leveled forests, animals reclaim habitats abandoned by humans, and satellites capture a new terrain free of its characteristic air and water pollution.

Perhaps this is the starting point.

Fractal geometry is at the heart of the natural world in the same way that Euclidian geometry anchors the man-made world. In the same way that it took centuries for us to look past what our own hands had made to see the natural world that surrounds us, so now we see past our own industry to glimpse what has always been right before our eyes. We see one another. We see possibility. We see new ways of knowing and being and understanding. And we seek more. We innovate. We reach. We reconsider.

There is no longer a status quo. Everything has changed. Everything is new.

When we produced the theater-dance collaboration *Fractals* in 2016, we were frustrated by the limitations of working in a festival environment, in a compressed time frame, with a limited budget, with so many restrictions on production values such as sets and lighting and sound. Adapting to these limitations, embracing what can be achieved with a small group of performers in an extremely streamlined capacity, may illustrate a first step we can take as a community towards rebuilding the public performance worlds of theater, music, and dance. Simplicity has become an asset. And simplicity need not limit the richness or the artistic satisfaction of our endeavors. Instead of dwelling on what we cannot do, we can make new discoveries based on what is available to us.

The world of education is no different. Simplicity has become an asset. Now more than ever, we can see the value of embracing what is essential. Everything extraneous fell away the first day students logged on instead of showing up. Educators are faced with the challenge of reaching students in new ways, of reimagining curricula. Perhaps this will propel us past rote learning and high stakes testing, the extraneous weight that has made teaching and learning a burden instead of a joy.

Perhaps we are in a unique position to ask ourselves how learning can emerge from inquiry and extend it; how we may construct knowledge together instead of transmitting it from one to another; how we can stop teasing the world apart into discrete bodies of knowledge and instead examine it in its complexity – in all the places where science and art and math and language and history intersect.

In their book *Collaboration in the Arts from the Middle Ages to the Present*, editors Silvia Bigliazzi and Sharon Wood compiled a challenging and compelling series of essays on the nature of collaboration. Many of the key concepts intrinsic to these essays align with the contents of *Fractals*. They define collaboration as "a joint effort between two parties achieving a result greater than or different from the sum of its parts." This definition is woven into the work that resulted in *Fractals*, in all its capacities, yet it was more than two parties from whom the work emerged. Far more.

Chapter 1: Origins

In Richard Littlejohns's essay on collaboration as ideology, he describes the phenomenon of abandoning ego out of mutual respect so that people might join efforts as co-creators, that they might value collective thought and creation above individual self-expression or artistic control. The origins of *Fractals* are rooted in choreographer Meredith Barnes's concept for the project, but equally in her openness to let it assume different shapes as other artists joined the work and as our understanding of the subject matter expanded. She set the tone for a project in which different artists would bring different sensibilities to the work, resulting in a work that was beyond what we could have predicted, designed, or constructed outside of the rehearsal room.

Chapter 2: Development

Enrico Giaccherini's essay examines the collaboration that transpires when one person builds on the work of a predecessor. Much of this project emerged from the notion of dancers and actors working together: merging the two art forms at times; at others, asking artists to explore the work through one another's craft. We modeled this conceptually on the work of productions that came before ours. The discovery of fractals themselves results from centuries of people picking up a thread of intellectual inquiry to see where it leads, realizing the work of those who came before them, and advancing that inquiry by degrees.

Chapter 3: The Text

Emily Eells identifies the collaboration between readers and writers as a "necessary complement." She describes the relationship as one consciousness existing with another, the two comprising separate halves of the same entity. The text of *Fractals* required several means of expression to align the writer with the reader: first the actors, then the audience, and ultimately the reader who holds this book. The work is explored through poetry, prose, and playwriting. In this edition, research writing is also employed. The text is annotated to provide the reader with information necessary to understand *Fractals* beyond its surface.

Chapter 4: Production

Carla Dente contributed an essay on the collaboration of text and performance in theater works. She discusses text transmission through the vehicle of theater, the various production elements (scenery, props, movement, music) serving to bridge the written and stage representations of a work. She posits that the work only acquires its full meaning if and when it is perceived in its completeness. *Fractals* was not complete until it was in performance in a particular venue, in this case one that required access to hearing, hard of hearing, and Deaf persons. The work of the creative team was incomplete without the production team, and this work was incomplete until it was put before an audience.

Chapter 5: Applications

Silvia Bigliazzi's essay describes the collaboration achieved through interaction among different media, or the combination of genres. When media are combined artistically, they can serve as an "intratextual mechanism" that conveys the work's meaning at its deepest levels. This chapter in *Fractals* presents a range of applications for this work and for works like it, beginning with a production history of theater-dance collaborations and extending beyond performance art into the worlds of writing and writing instruction, and education (arts education, academics, STEAM and other forms of interdisciplinary education).

Our hope is that this book would serve as both a resource and an inspiration. As we all move forward into a world of perpetual re-invention, shifting sensibilities, evolving aesthetics, and changing demands, we depend on collaboration and innovation to move us forward. The world of fractals is an invisible world made visible, a world that surrounds us that we did not know existed, a world of continual discoveries built on the knowledge and wonder of those who came before us. This is a world that can open us to possibilities, to new ideas, to solutions.

CHAPTER 1

ORIGINS

Fractals are patterns, infinitely reiterating, self-similar in shape. Benoit Mandelbrot coined the term in the 1970s, but scientists and mathematicians had been exploring the concept for centuries. Mandelbrot developed a geometry to express things found in the natural rather than the man-made world – coastlines, galaxies, anatomy, clouds, trees, snowflakes, honeycombs, etc. Fractals are intrinsic to Chaos Theory – the science of surprises, of the non-linear and unpredictable. They reveal the order governing the seemingly chaotic in our world. As we learn to recognize them, we gain insight into our world, our selves, one another.

This was the introduction that appeared in our program for the Summer 2016 performances of *Fractals*, but I could not have written it four months earlier. When Meredith Barnes first spoke to me about collaborating on this project, I had only a vague idea of what a fractal was. I knew it had to do with shape. I certainly didn't realize that fractals surround us, that they live inside us. As my research unfolded, I became fascinated by the spirituality embedded in their existence. They are there whether we see them or not, seemingly random yet so complex as to be impossible without the divine touch, an omniscient design.

Equally fascinating is the way that men came to the edge of discovering this phenomenon for centuries without being able to realize it. Because of the need to compute thousands of equations to replicate the patterns of self-similarity and fractal dimension, history had to wait for technology to catch up to the natural world. As computer technology advanced, Mandelbrot was able to compute the mathematics of the Julia Set, graph the data, and watch with wonder as images emerged. The Mandelbrot set was an extension of this work and exploded an awareness of fractals into the public consciousness and the popular culture.

The images we associate with the Mandelbrot Set, the Julia Set, and others emerge from plotting the data on a graph, then reiterating those numbers by hundreds and thousands of times. (https://fractaltodesktop.com/mandelbrot-set-basics/index.html provides an excellent step by step explanation of this with illustations.)

Now we extend Mandelbrot's work into problem solving that includes diagnosing cancer in its earliest stages; addressing global warming by understanding the relationship of the rain forest to rising

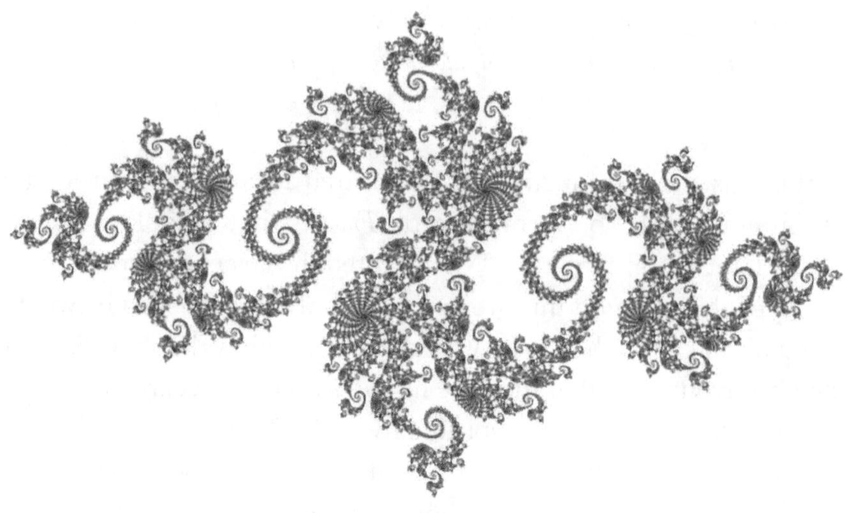

Julia Set

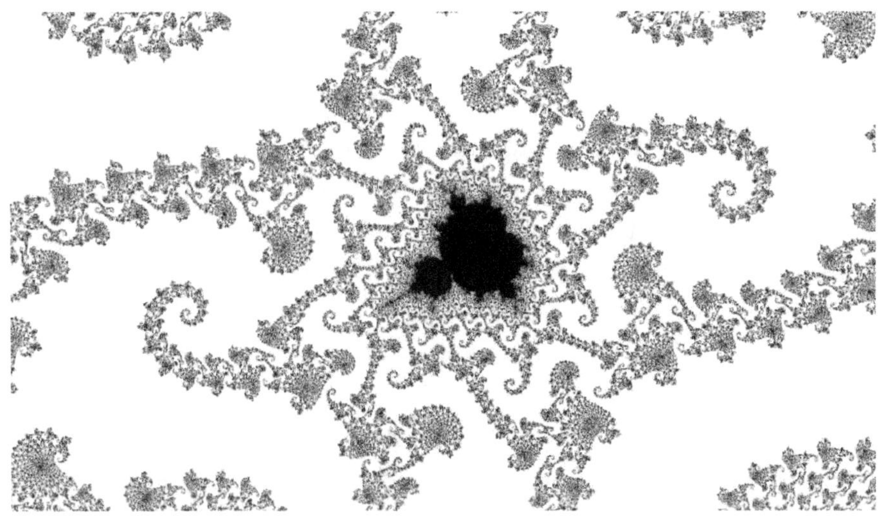

Mandelbrot Set

CO2 levels; expanding the boundaries of CGI in creating special effects for filmmaking; analyzing financial markets; and countless other worlds. The applications are endless, limited only to our understanding and imagination.

> *"Look! Life is only comprehensible through a thousand local gods. And not just the old dead ones with names like Zeus – no, but living Geniuses of Place and Person! And not just Greece but modern England! Spirits of certain trees, certain curves of brick wall, certain fish and chip shops, if you like, and slate roofs – just as of certain frowns of people and slouches . . . I'd say to them – 'Worship as many as you see and more will appear!'"*

—Peter Shaffer, *Equus*

Worship as many as you see and more will appear. The more aware you are of the branching patterns of trees, the presence of the Fibonacci sequence in seashells and plant life, the self-similarity in the clouds above your head or the waves that wash over your feet, the more you will see. As James Brown of the University of New Mexico describes it, it is an invisible world made visible.

In the spring of 2016, Meredith asked to speak with me about a project she was developing. She had several dance pieces, some that had already been performed and some that were still works-in-progress. She had made a commitment to perform in the Capital Fringe Festival (Washington, D.C.) that summer, but she needed the dance pieces to become a piece of theater. She knew that the thread that could run through all of them thematically was fractals.

Meredith had a piece in development called *Fractals*, (built on the counts of the Fibonacci sequence rather than the meter of the music she was using) as well as one she had performed called *Sea Glass* (which captured the fractal nature of the movement of waves, the patterns of turbulence, the fractal design of sea life) and another called *Inconscient* (which, among other things, captured the fractal patterns typical of the movement of crowds).

I had seen productions where actors dance and dancers act and thought we might be able to create a similar dynamic as a means of conveying information about fractals, about the content of the dance pieces, and about the meaning we were making of that — meaning specific to the work and beyond the work.

I asked where her thinking began on this project, what had made her aware of fractals and interested in exploring them through dance. She had come across an article describing Bartholomäus Traubeck's work in which he developed a method to "play" slices of tree trunk as though they were phonograph records, translating the rings into music. This served as a launch pad for us, common ground, a firm footing that could send us into the directions and connections and discoveries this work would require. (It is worth mentioning here that Meredith decided to stage the beginning and end of this dance solo on a turntable made from a slice of tree

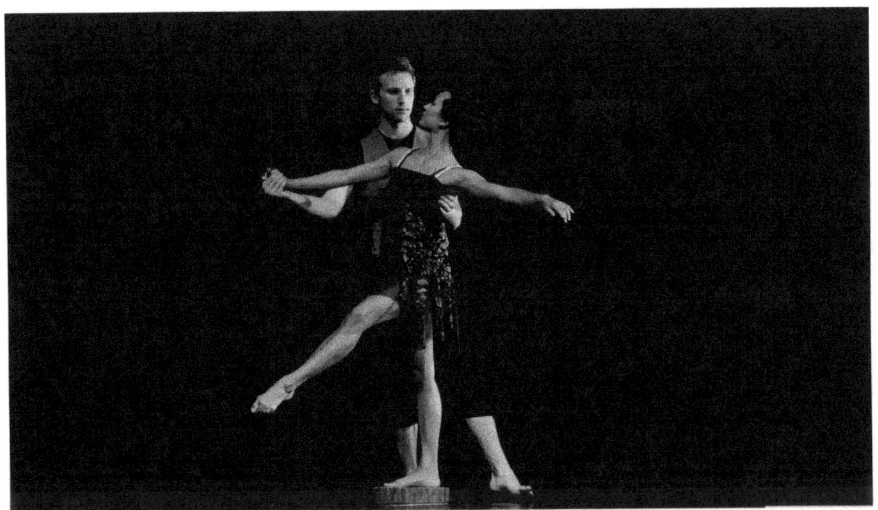

Dancing on a turntable, inspired by Traubeck
Photo credit: Ruth Judson

trunk, a beautiful homage to Traubeck's innovation and its role as our impetus.)

I had seen some of the pieces before, but I asked Meredith to articulate what she was saying in each of the five dance pieces she was planning for the show, and to start linking those ideas to the world of fractals. I wanted to distill this into themes and begin to think about using actors and/or multimedia to move the project more towards theater and away from dance concert. This is, by the way, a rare privilege – to hear a choreographer articulate what a given work means to her. I had read the pieces differently, although my understanding was not in conflict with her intentions. Asking her to unpack the meaning made my understanding richer.

Meredith's guiding concepts were as follows:

Inconscient There is hidden dimension. There is much we are unaware of. Busyness, multi-tasking, being distracted by our own little worlds. We miss life happening around us.

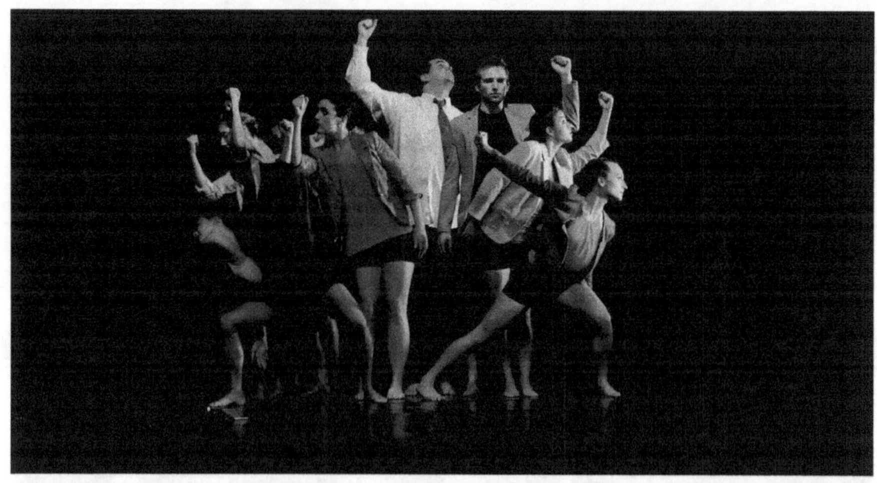

Inconscient
Photo credit: Ruth Judson

Fractals Fractals give us a way to see the invisible. Mandelbrot's work shows smooth shapes broken into pieces, reiterating, self-similar shapes repeating in different ways and different scales to show something larger and seemingly new.

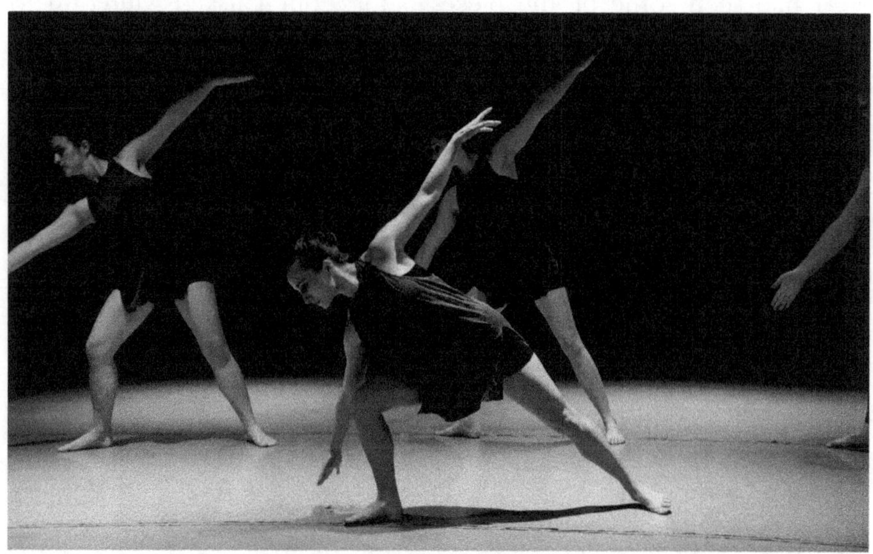

Fractals
Photo credit: Ruth Judson

Cord of Three Strands In our attempt to make sense of a chaotic world, fractals give us comfort that there is order when we feel none. This reflects human behavior and relationships. Connectedness gives us strength and makes us feel that we are not alone.

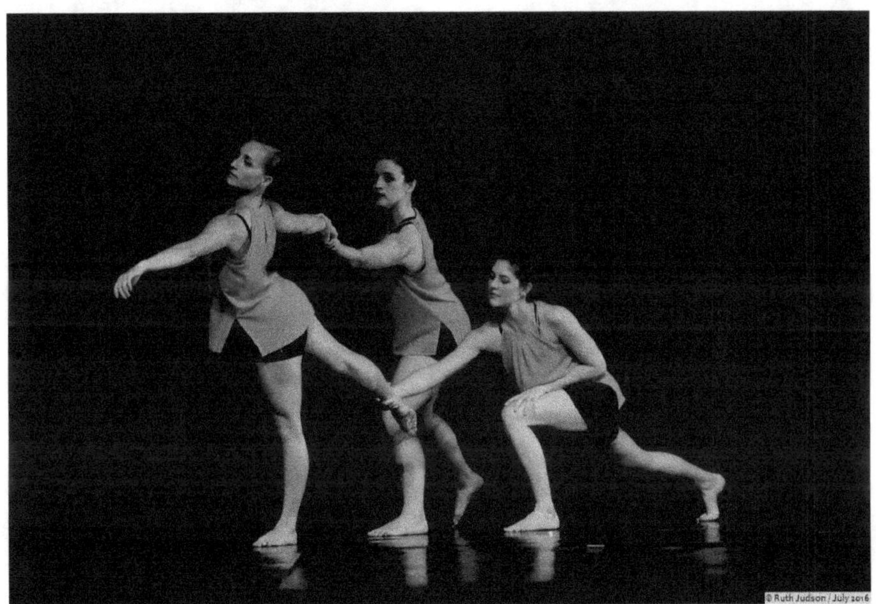

Cord of Three Strands
Photo credit: Ruth Judson

Solo Fractals connect human bodies to the physical world. The same geometry that is found in trees is in our bodies. Dance can be used to express these connections. Art, math, and science can say the same things; they just speak different languages.

Sea Glass Even turbulence is a beautiful fractal phenomenon. You can see it in the ocean with the help of colorful algae blooms. In the same way, waves shape and form broken glass into something beautiful.

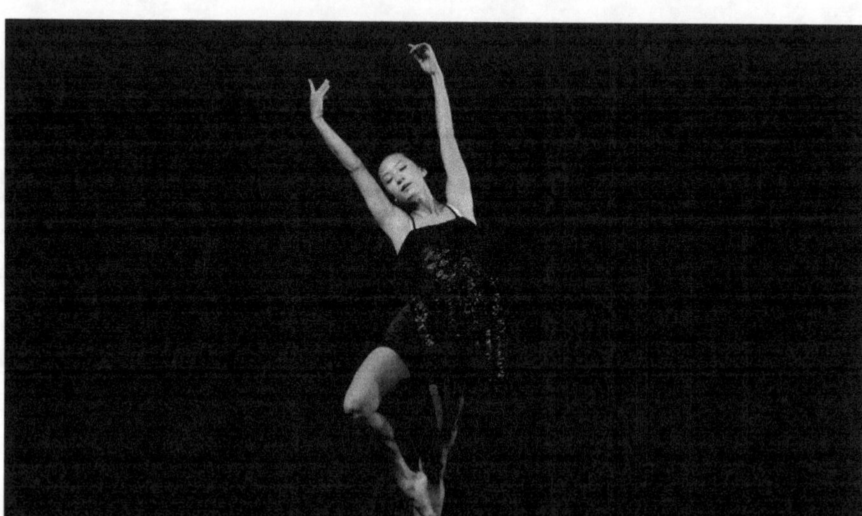

Solo
Photo credit: Ruth Judson

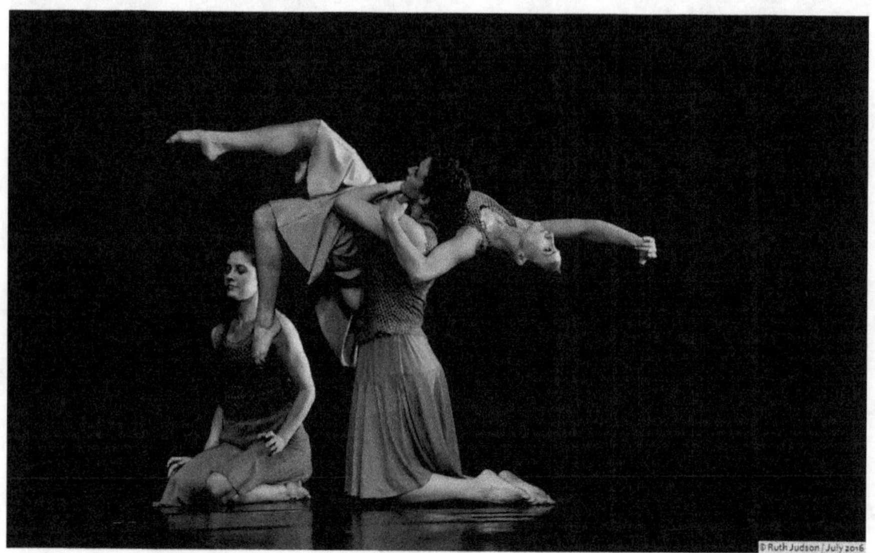

Sea Glass
Photo credit: Ruth Judson

We ultimately decided against multimedia because of the time constraint we were facing. It would be a fascinating option should we have the opportunity to re-mount the show at some future date. There are so many possibilities. From Meredith's conceptualization, I created four guiding ideas:

- **Fractals represent an invisible world that is right before our eyes**. This world is present in all its complexity whether we know it is there or acknowledge its existence. We miss many things or take them for granted because we don't know — or notice.

- **The logic and design of fractals helps us make sense of a chaotic world.** Our brains seek patterns to make sense of the world — beneficial ways, like fractals, and potentially harmful ones, like stereotyping. Our human effort to organize a world that is too vast to contain and make meaning of it is never ending, as are fractals. Our understanding of the world changes and reiterates, continually, as do fractals.

- **These concepts are reflected by human behavior and relationships.** We encounter one another and try to make, keep, and restore order among ourselves. What we think we see blinds us to the hidden things that are right in front of us — often in those we love most and think we know best.

- **Fractals connect the human body to the physical world** (e.g. the branches of trees and the branches of the circulatory system, the structure of the lungs). Dance is the body's art form; dance and movement are ways to interpret and express these connections.

I began to hear these ideas unfolding in my mind in the form of spoken word poetry. Spoken word is often misunderstood, as is slam poetry. It has a reputation for being strident, militant, overdramatic. It is not, necessarily. At its most essential, it is writing for the stage rather than the page. We needed to cast actors to deliver this material at the beginning of the show and between the dance pieces; we wanted actors who could move, who could more than move, who would be willing to dance. We wanted movement to illustrate the words the actors were speaking, and for actors and dancers to be onstage together creating transitions and weaving the spoken and danced material into a unified statement.

In addition to the time constraint of the production period, we faced the time constraint of the show itself. The Capital Fringe Festival had allotted us 50 minutes. Because this was a festival performance the running time was quite firm, with only 15 minutes to load in and 15 minutes to strike each show.

We invited choreographer Amanda Whiteman to join us. Her style was similar to Meredith's, and I needed someone with a solid background in modern dance to help me discover ways to use the body to illustrate the complex ideas we would be asking our audience to grasp in a brief period of time.

During the auditions we decided to cast actors of significantly different ages. We cast two teenage boys and two actors in their 30s (one male, one female) all of whom had strong theater backgrounds and some dance experience. We approached a number of men and women in their 50s but could not find actors who were willing to take company class with Meredith's company, Dance Art Theater, and move to the extent that we envisioned. We wanted one man and one woman in this age range. We ended up with me. The mission of Dance Art Theater is rooted in diversity. We wanted this value to be reflected in the cast. We also wanted to say something visually about the body as it ages, its relationship to its younger iterations, its capacity to integrate with the world around it at any age and stage.

We were assigned a performance space at Gallaudet University, a federally chartered private university for the education of the Deaf and hard of hearing, located in Washington, D.C. We were required by the festival organizers to make our performances accessible to

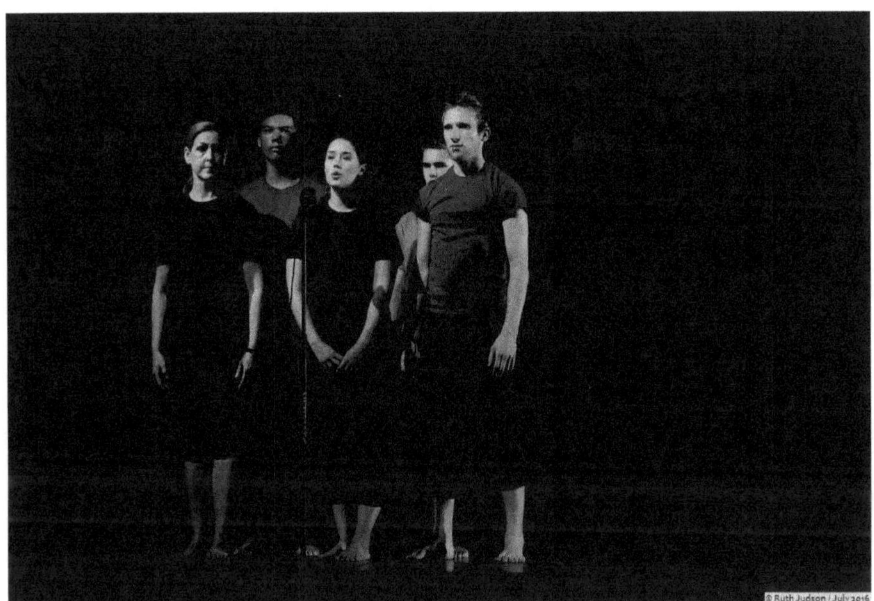

Cast of *Fractals*
Photo credit: Ruth Judson

the community through closed captioning of the text. In addition, Meredith had a dancer in her company who is Deaf and who layered some sign language into the choreography, specifically for the piece *Inconscient*. Given more time we would love to have set some of the text in sign language. We explored that option, but it was not feasible in a six-week rehearsal period during which time the text would be under revision and choreography would be built on the actors as they worked.

Our first meeting about this project was in early March 2016. I spent a month meeting with Meredith and doing extensive research, and then another month writing. I wrote the first draft in spoken word poetry. I adapted this to a scripted version in which the text was divided among different speakers. I completed an additional draft, adapted to prose, during the rehearsal period – the meaning of the text needed to be clearer to the actors.

Drafting the poetic lines as prose helped them to find whole ideas and the rhythms more typical of conversational speech. I based this approach on an exercise I learned as a young actor, to study a monologue by writing it out with no punctuation. The punctuation is critically important, but removing it allows the words to become tools that can be adapted to purpose and action, to the truth of the moment, and it allows different meanings to emerge. The punctuation is layered back in afterwards.

I also amplified this draft; the actors had been given some dramaturgical background before and during rehearsals, but there were still gaps in their understanding. This book includes all three versions: poetry, scripted poetry, and scripted prose. The amplified version has been set on the performance script in Chapter 3 ***The Text***.

As of June, we had a cast, several dance pieces, a working script, and six weeks. We had a lot of work ahead of us, exciting work, a new world to discover and explore.

CHAPTER 2

DEVELOPMENT

Several productions preceded ours in experimenting with the notion of combining actors and dancers onstage in such a way that each shared the others' role, with actors dancing and dancers acting, beyond the ways they typically incorporate the two art forms in their work.

Susan Stroman and John Weidman's 2000 Broadway musical *Contact* carried the award season of that year. It is composed of three dance pieces, spanning three different time periods and locations, threaded on the theme of making contact – or failing to – within and across relationships. The cast was comprised of triple threat performers with strong backgrounds in theater and dance.

Susan Shields and Heather McDonald's 2011 *Stay* spent two years in development and was performed at several D.C. area venues (Theater of the First Amendment, Woolly Mammoth, The Lansburgh Theater). This production explicitly asked its actors to dance and its dancers to act to an extent that I have not seen elsewhere. The dance pieces functioned as scene work in a scripted text chronicling a multigenerational family as it copes with change across time.

There is a rich history of professional works that explore the relationship of movement to text, productions in which dance comprises and advances a narrative. These are explored in more depth in Chapter 5 ***Applications.***

Our intention when we set out was closest to the approach employed in *Stay*, of having actors dance and dancers act. We did not accomplish this to the degree we hoped. It is a lot to ask of each type of artist, not only to explore the world of someone else's art but to gain competence in it to the extent that it is ready for an audience.

What we were able to do was create a story world in which the narrative traveled through words and movement, and in which actors and dancers inhabited one another's worlds. Actors were choreographed on a given piece of text, dancers joined the scene created by the text and created transitions into the dance pieces, actors were incorporated into dance pieces, images in the text were staged on members of the cast and members of the dance company, each echoing the other. Music and sound were used to bridge these transitions.

Through it all, there was a strong narrative running through each dance piece and running through the production as a whole. While perhaps not what we initially envisioned, and not what we would do in the next iteration, it was extremely satisfying work. It has opened a door to a realm of new possibilities.

THE DANCERS

Meredith Barnes

Meredith had read about Bartholomäus Traubeck's work, developing laser technology that could translate information from tree rings into music. She knew she wanted to set material on this music. She began to read and learn about fractals. As with most people, once she knew what they were she started seeing them everywhere. She started to build a dance, *Fractals*, exploring it in the studio, expanding on the concept.

Unlike many choreographers who "see it when they hear it" as Meredith says, she typically works from a concept rather than music. She explores the idea with her dancers, experimenting, discovering phrases, ordering the narrative and creating transitions later in the process. The Traubeck music was not a fit for the dance that was emerging, so she put it aside for later.

Fractals

Where a choreographer working from music would count based on the meter of the piece, Meredith used the Fibonacci sequence as counts, highlighting those numbers as they occur in the

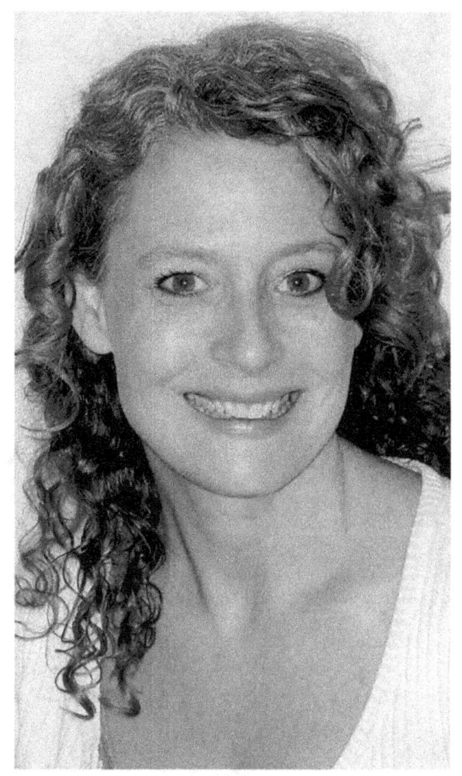

Meredith Barnes
Photo credit: Kelly Jones

movement, assigning dancers to particular Fibonacci numbers so that they always move on a given count. Many of the phrases in the piece were based on visual images found in nature – spirals, mountaintops – places where the Fibonacci sequence exists in the natural world. She wanted to make the mathematics something everyone could relate to, and felt nature was an easier pathway for most people than math; warmer, more accessible, part of our everyday lives, part of our bodies. Having completed *Fractals*, she began to wonder how other pieces she had done could fit thematically, how more dances could be created to make an entire show.

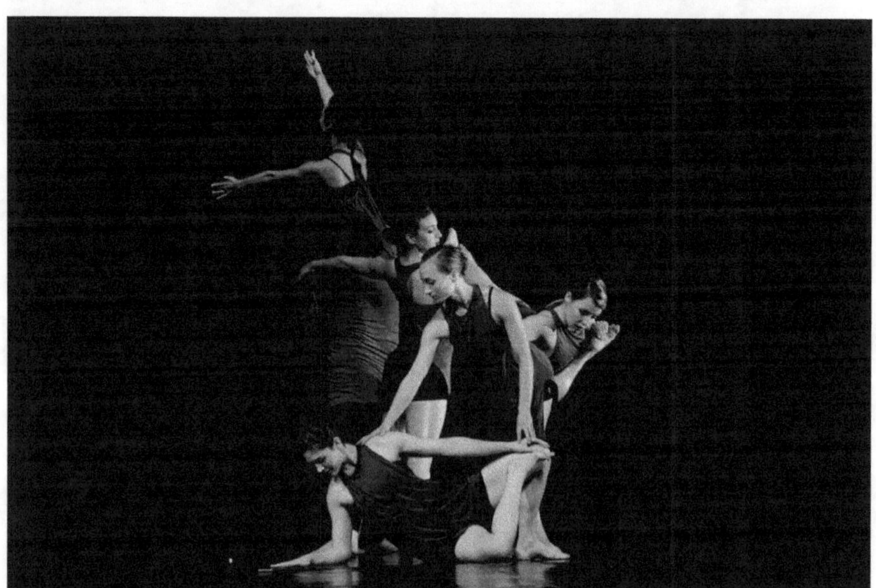

Fractals
Photo credit: Ruth Judson

Solo

Working from the concept of fractals being part of human physiology and anatomy – and working from the music Traubeck captured from tree rings on his 2012 album, *Years* – Meredith created a piece with dancer Darian Iida to personify both. In one exploration, they rolled a die which corresponded to different movement – stretch, jump, travel – plugging the number on the die into an algorithm to expand the work.

While she feels that people see and interpret a dance according to their own experience, Meredith intended several representations to manifest in this dance. One, that Darian would be the music that comes from the tree, and that her entrance would signify that music is everywhere and that nature ultimately is its source. Two, that our bodies are fractals and are intertwined with the natural world and the man-made expressions of it (such as music and dance). In this dance,

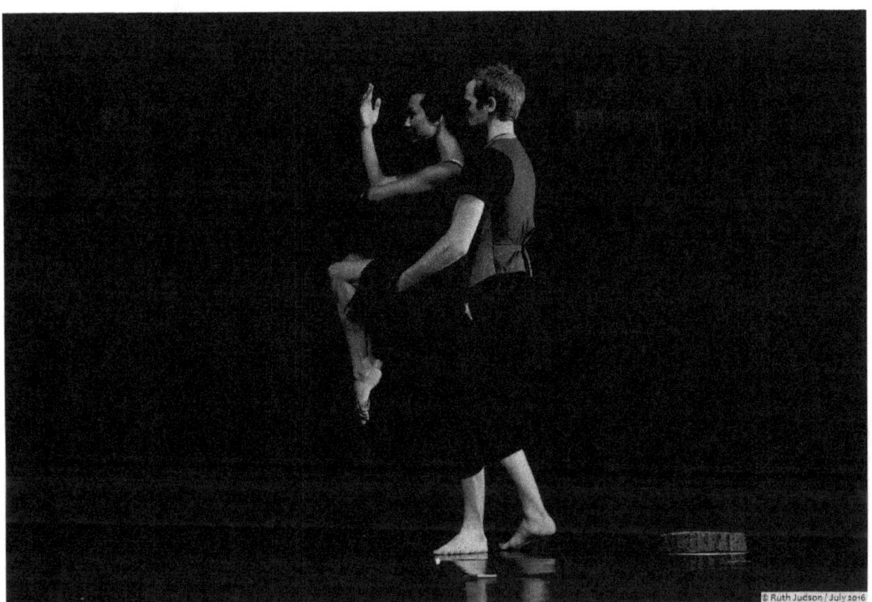

Solo

Photo credit: Ruth Judson

Darian is carried in by one of the actors and placed on a slice of tree trunk, mounted on a turntable. Her dance begins and ends with this profound visual statement.

Inconscient

This piece is focused more on the relational aspect of fractals than mathematics or patterns, the ways we are so caught up in our own worlds that we don't see the people around us whose lives are as vivid as our own. Meredith read an anecdote in Heather Zempel's *Amazed and Confused* in which Zempel relates her ordeal of walking home from work one evening – a seven-minute walk from an advisory position with the U.S. Senate to her home on Capitol Hill – and falling into a seven-foot sinkhole. The ground crumbled beneath her feet at the corner of 2nd and F Streets in Washington D.C. during rush hour. She tried to escape, she yelled for help, she called her husband and got his voice mail, she used her umbrella to try to catch someone's attention.

Nothing worked.

Not only did Meredith want to capture this narrative, she wanted to explore the way that time stands still in a crisis, a woman frozen in time in the midst of a bustling crowd. The piece resolves with the crowd crossing the stage to include someone left behind, a reminder that we can choose to see the needs of those around us anywhere and at any moment.

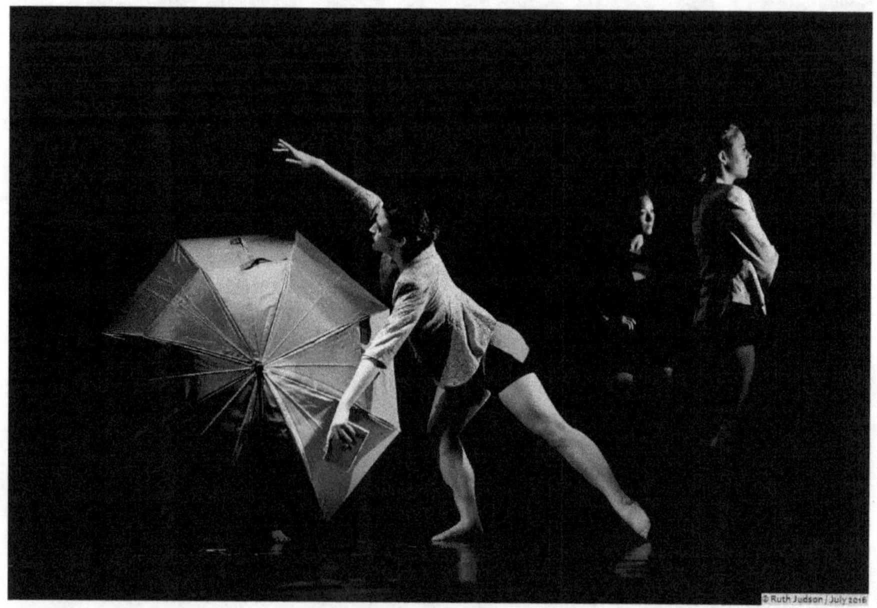

Inconscient
Photo credit: Ruth Judson

Cord of Three Strands

This was one of the first pieces Meredith choreographed for Dance Art Theater after founding the company in 2014. She felt strongly about including it on this program because of the strong statement it makes that as human beings we are all connected to one another, and we need connection. The biblical allusion is to our being stronger together than we are alone.

This was one of the pieces where the actors and dancers mirrored one another to create a transition between the text and the dance, and in doing so underlined Meredith's intended meaning. She also remarked that this was one of the places in the show where the text brought the dance to life and influenced the way in which these dancers performed work already familiar to them. The intersection of text and movement deepened the dancers understanding of the piece and added new layers of meaning, which informed their performance of it.

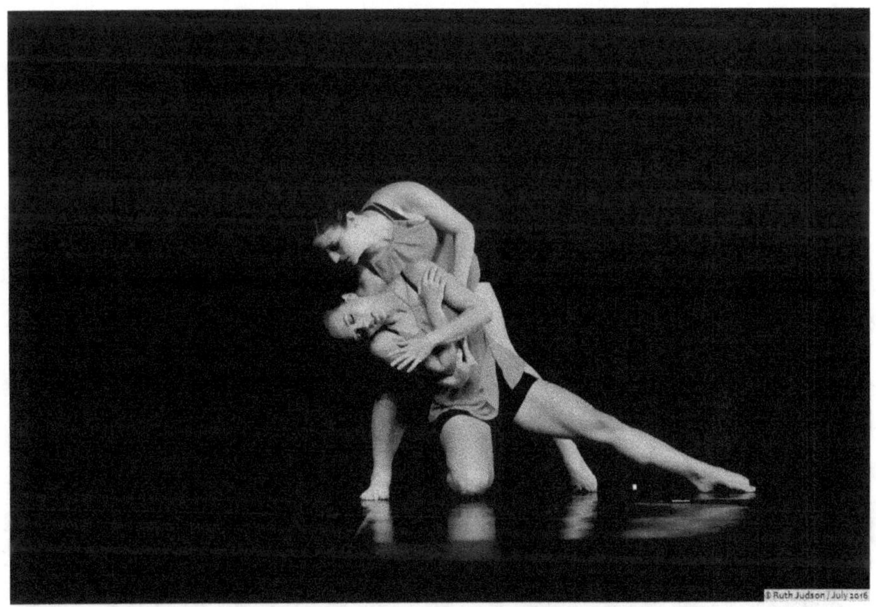

Cord of Three Strands
Photo credit: Ruth Judson

Sea Glass

This piece had also been performed by Dance Art Theater previously, but Meredith made a thematic connection to the fractal phenomenon underlying the Koch snowflake and the way it has been used to measure irregular shapes such as coastlines. Tides, shells, and sea life are also fractals and many bear a relation to the Fibonacci sequence. (This is explained in more detail in the annotated version of the script in Chapter 3.)

In describing this piece, Meredith underscored the notion that she typically works from a thematic concept rather than a narrative. What tends to emerge from the work is more message than story, a message open to the meaning the audience members make. In this piece she shows that something can undergo turbulent change to become something else, trash to treasure, a man-made object returned to the natural world and transformed by it. She makes visual statements that this process is painful, difficult, and awkward, but that it yields a thing of beauty.

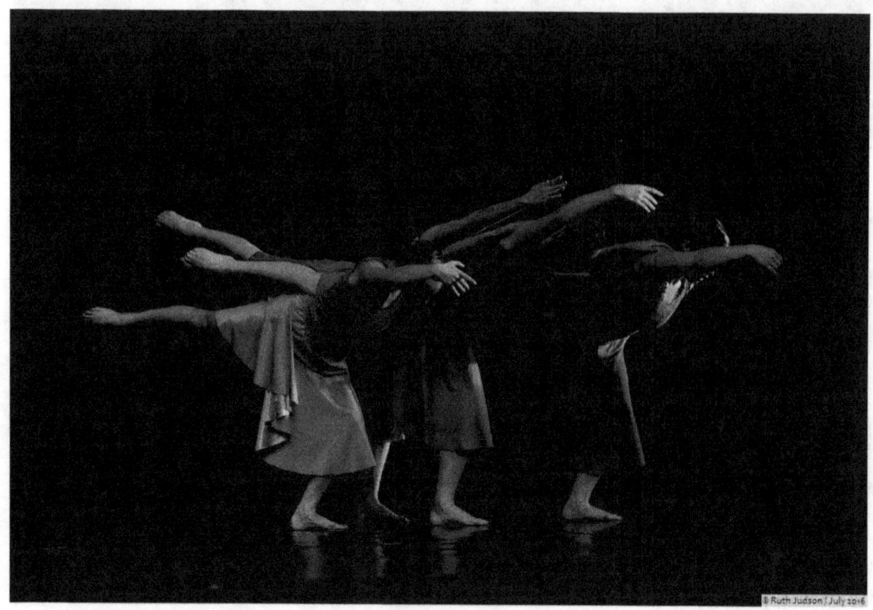

Sea Glass
Photo credit: Ruth Judson

THE MOVEMENT: *Amanda Whiteman*

Amanda and I had several creative interactions before *Fractals*. We met working on a show together in 2012 for which she was the choreographer. She heads a dance studio and company called Groundshare Arts Alliance. Her company performed at a fundraiser that I produced, so I was familiar with her style. We needed someone to set the text in motion, someone to create movement for the actors that would dovetail with the work Meredith was creating. Amanda proved to be a perfect match.

She felt, from the beginning of this collaboration, that her work was to build a bridge between the text and the dances, between my work with the actors and Meredith's work with the dancers. She was looking for a way to create connection between the two worlds that would allow us all to traverse them, to travel back and forth between them, to inhabit one another's worlds. She watched Meredith work, and she built her physical vocabulary on what she saw in the dance rehearsals.

As she describes it, she started from the text. Her intention was to explore the piece conceptually through movement that would resemble Meredith's, break the concepts into smaller pieces, find images that would convey those concepts to the audience, and find the actions and motivations to compel and propel the actors' movement.

Because Amanda speaks the languages of both modern dance and theater dance, she was able to stand

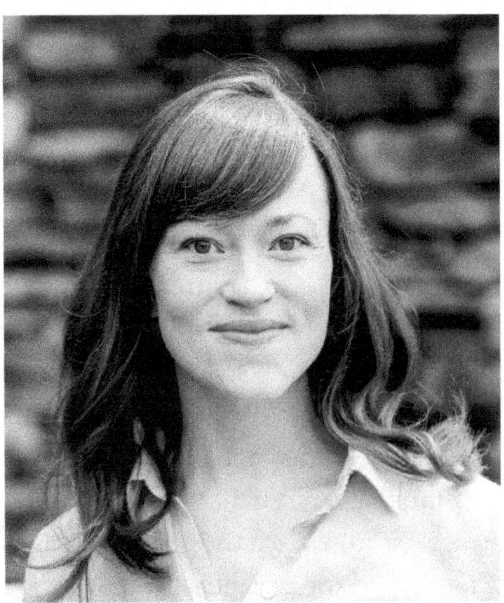

Amanda Whiteman

Photo credit: Angelina Namkung, copyright Wolf Trap

in the gap between actors and dancers quite ably – although she would be the first to tell you that the work was entirely based on trial and error. She was facing two obstacles: One, the degree to which the actors were comfortable with movement and with physically connecting with one another; and two, the physical limitation imposed on us by the performance space and the availability of only one standing microphone.

In an ideal world, the sound design would have allowed us to speak and move simultaneously. As it was, we always had to have speakers anchored to the microphone while those not speaking came and went, speaking first then moving, joining together in choral speech, and peeling off to illustrate the complex ideas conveyed by the text.

Amanda also would have preferred to have more options than the minimal lighting plot a festival environment allows. Lighting, sound, language, and motion have the potential to converge powerfully into story. However, a festival setting does not allow the time to load the equipment in and out, nor the rehearsal time to set and rehearse its use.

I agree with her that I would welcome an opportunity to realize this production more completely, yet I think the simple design environment showcases the artistic product beautifully by isolating it. The whole task of conveying story, character, and concepts rooted in mathematics and quantum physics had to be accomplished solely through language, movement, and music. We found this frustrating at times, yet artistically gratifying.

Amanda was the most satisfied by two aspects of the finished product. One was that the movement and dance were successful at educating our audience, at embodying and communicating complex ideas to them in accessible ways. The other was the degree to which there was seamless transition and connection between the actors and the dancers: such as the incorporation of actors into the dances, *Inconscient* and *Solo*; the mirror images created in the spoken piece, *Fractals*; and the transitions into *Cord of Three Strands* and *Sea Glass*.

In a future production, our actors would dance more, speaking while they are in motion. Our dancers would speak as well as move.

Ideally, it would be difficult to classify the company as actors and dancers, because they would occupy more of the same stage time and be blended more completely into one another's story worlds.

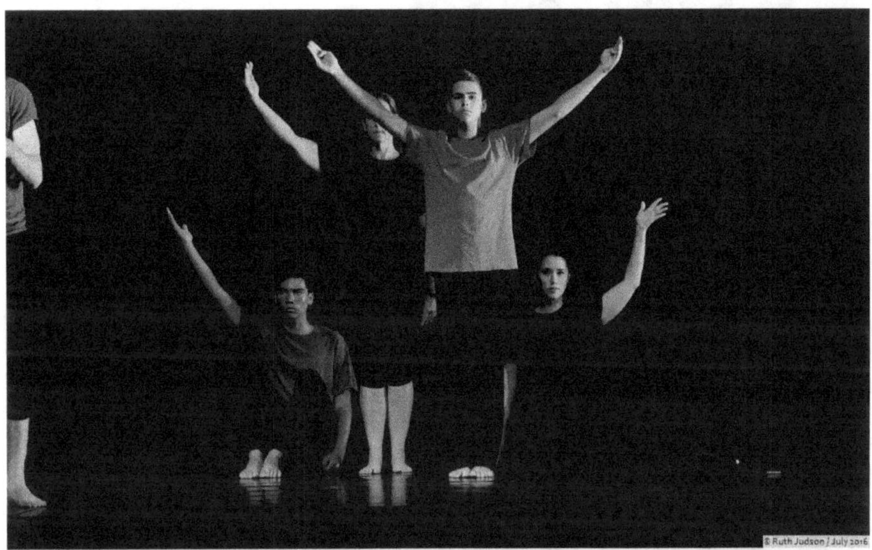

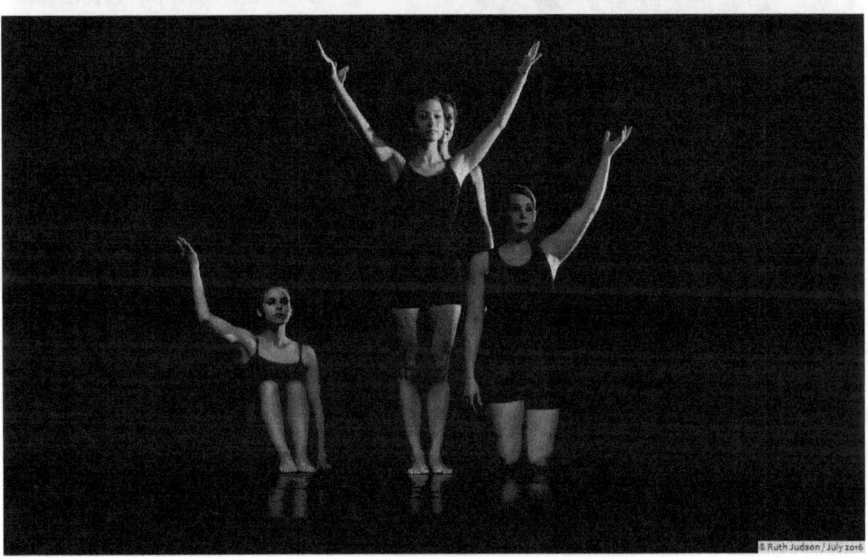

Mirror images of a cluster of trees
Photo credit: Ruth Judson

THE ACTORS

Kimberley Cetron

Kimberley Cetron
Photo credit: Julie Napear Photography

The first challenge was casting actors who were willing to take risks, working not primarily through their minds and emotions but equally through their bodies. It was important to this production — because of the nature of the work and the extreme time constraint — that they be willing to take company class with Dance-ArtTheater, which Meredith was holding weekly just before our mutual rehearsal time.

During other rehearsals, the dancers and actors worked separately. I have always found it amusing that casting calls for musicals are designated for "dancers" and "singers who move." No one in the professional world assumes that a dancer can sing or that a singer can dance, although there are many who do. Similarly, actors tend to be more cerebral and emotional than physical — and these actors would need to be willing to take class alongside professional dancers.

We were extremely fortunate to find two teenage boys and two thirty-something actors. We also wanted an older man and woman but could find no one. I stepped in, rather than lose this dynamic in the work. While not ideal, it did create some images worthy of contemplation: the body as it ages from teen age through young adulthood to middle age; teenage boys dancing alongside an adult male; a young woman dancing alongside an older woman; a mother and son dancing together.

The single biggest challenge was in the communication of the text. First, there is a tendency to read poetry for style rather than for meaning. Second, there is a tendency to give an emotional reading rather than trusting that the meaning will emerge from one's purpose in speaking it. Finally, with regard to this text, it was imperative that we communicate a challenging set of ideas and concepts to an audience we assumed to know as little about fractals as we did when we started the work.

I had written the original text in spoken word poetry. Once we finalized the cast, I formatted it as a script, some lines belonging to a single actor, some delivered chorally. At one of our final rehearsals before going into tech week, I found the meaning still unclear in places. I drafted a script copy written in prose rather than poetry and annotated the lines and phrases that were not operating as clearly as I thought they needed to for an audience new to the subject. This helped a great deal, but it was not a magic bullet. We continued to work on phrasing, meaning, clarity, and intention through the rehearsal period and each of the performances.

What follows are the three versions of the text: the spoken word version, the prose version, and the performance script. The performance script is the one that has been annotated here, for ease of reading and use. The prose version is offered simply as a model, as a problem-solving approach, and as an example of revising a text for a purpose (in this case, to streamline phrasing and clarify meaning for the actors so that the meaning they conveyed would, in turn, be clear).

CHAPTER 3

THE TEXT

1 – INTRODUCTION

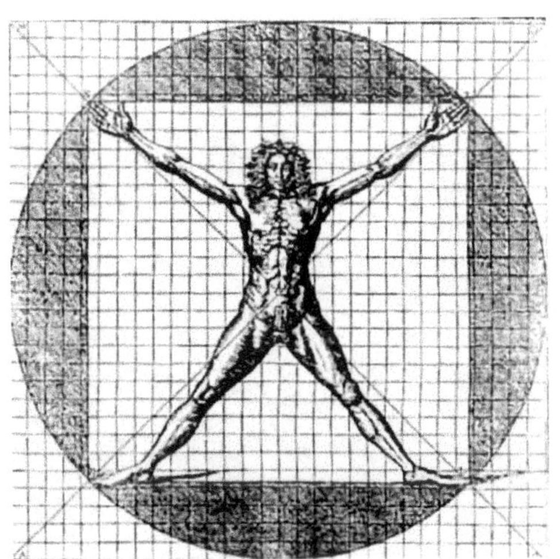

The Vitruvian Man, Vitruvius

1490

Leonardo da Vinci

Realizing the work

Of an ancient architect

Making mathematics visible

Blending art and science

Geometry and human proportion

Recognizing the divine

The length of the arms equal to a person's height

From knee to foot

From elbow to fingertip

One quarter of a person's height

A golden ratio

Evidence of a plan

Amid the chaos of being human

2000 years previous

Pythagoras

Used the circle to represent the spiritual realm

The square, the material world

da Vinci

Saw them as one

And if the human form

Then so the universe

1202

Leonardo Bonacci

Realizing the work

Of ancient India

Making mathematics visible

Studying population

Multiplying rabbits

Finding a solution

In a sequence of numbers

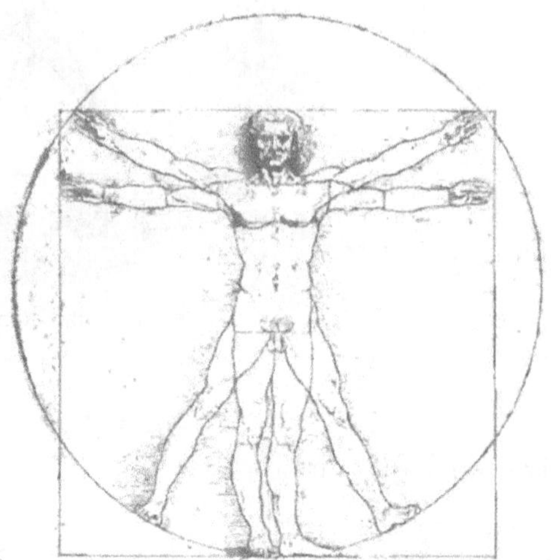

Vitruvian Man, da Vinci

0 and 1…1
1 and 1…2
1 and 2…3
2 and 3…5
3 and 5…8
5 and 8…13
8 and13…21…

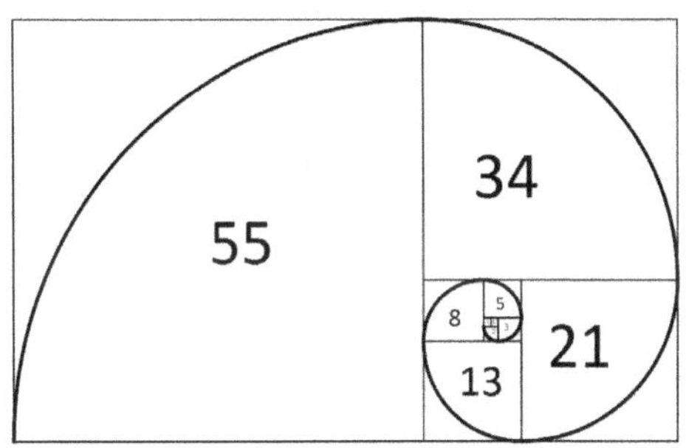

Fibonacci spiral/Golden ratio

Plants innately know

To flower this way

To blossom

To branch

Pinecones and pineapples

Sunflowers

Spiralize into this sequence

Knowing no math

Knowing only efficiency

Knowing how to

Flourish

The starfish, the nautilus shell

Our lungs, our blood vessels

We thrive and survive in these numbers

1883

Georg Cantor

Realizing the work

Of one of his contemporaries

Making mathematics visible

Dropped the middle third of a line

And the middle third of the remaining lines

And the middle third of those

Repeating

Infinitely

The Perfect Set

Cantor Set

1904

Helge von Koch

Realizing the work

Of Georg Cantor

Making mathematics visible

Devises a curve

Composed of straight lines

Infinitely long

Yet finite in its area

A pathological shape

A snowflake

An idea evolving through time

From before 1202…to 1490…1883…1904…

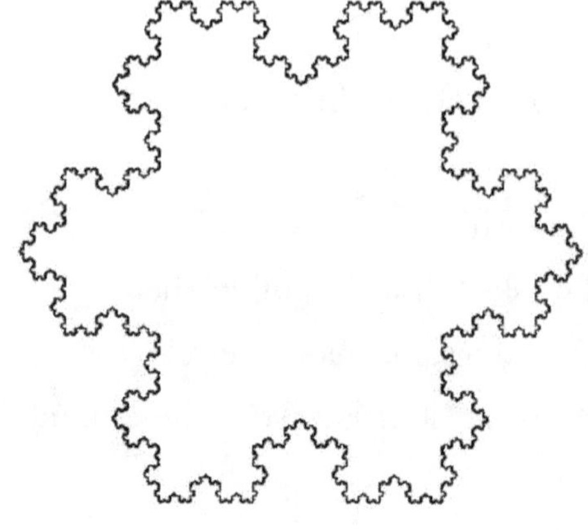

Koch snowflake

1980
Benoit Mandelbrot
Realizing the work
Of Julia and Fatou
The mathematicians
Of his youth
Exploding the limits
Of nature
Of art
Of music
Of architecture
Biology
Medicine
Finance
Mathematics
Making it visible
Giving it a name

Fractals
Patterns of shapes
Self-same shapes
Differing only in size
In scale
Repeating
Reiterating
All around us
Before Mandelbrot

Before Koch

Before Cantor

Before Fibonacci

da Vinci

Vitruvius

Pythagoras

The invisible world made visible

We do not see them into being

They are there

They wait to be known

2 – INCONSCIENT

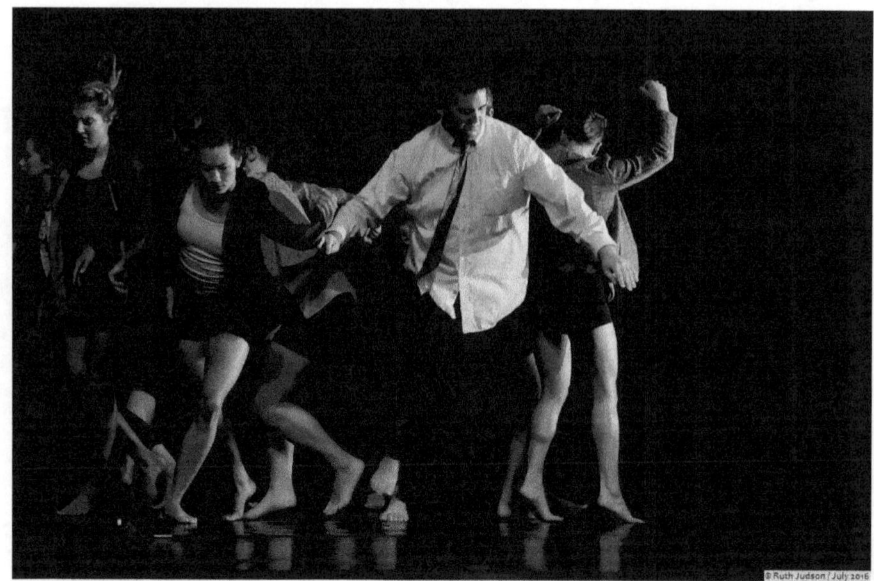

"We move with the crowd, an organism, a fractal."
Photo credit: Ruth Judson

We miss what surrounds us
Right before our eyes
A world that exists
In all its complexity
Whether we know it
Or see it
Or acknowledge it

Inconscient
Mindless
Distracted
Preoccupied
A world in motion
Frenetic
Chaotic

We could go in any direction
we choose
Yet we move with the crowd
An organism
A fractal

Rush hour
A woman finds herself
Seven feet underground
Suddenly
A sinkhole
Alone

Helpless

No reply

From the hundreds

Just above

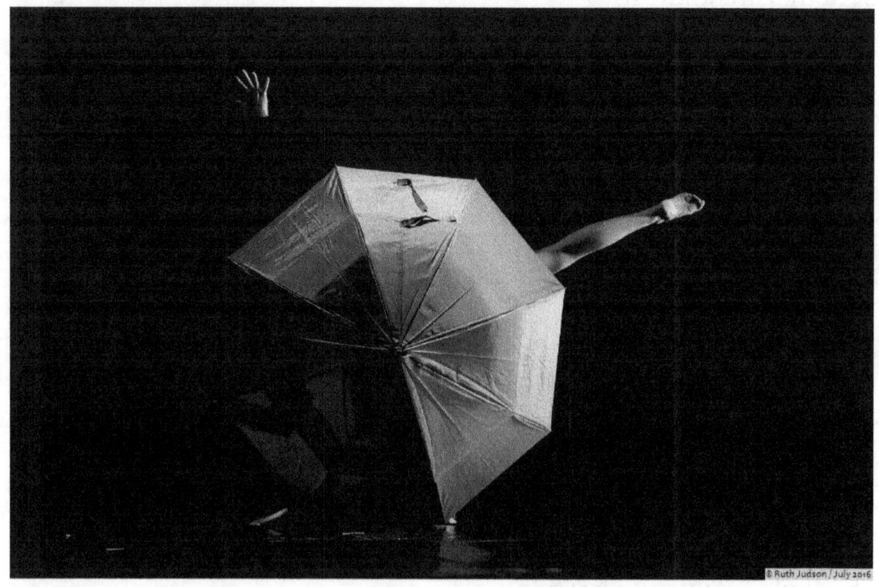

"We miss what surrounds us, right before our eyes."
Photo credit: Ruth Judson

She raises an umbrella

No response

She waits for rescue

We miss what surrounds us

Right before our eyes

We don't know to look

We don't stop to notice

3 – CORD OF THREE STRANDS

Fractals
Their logic, design
Attraction
Is their power
They provide
Order, sense
Safety
In a world that looks
On its surface
Tumultuous, disordered

Pollock understood
Layering paint
Imitating nature
Adopting its dynamics
Van Gogh captured
The patterns in the turbulence
Rather than the
Darkness of the night
Hokusai saw
The crest of the wave
Not its danger
The wings of a bird
Not its distance
We seek a language
To make sense from confusion

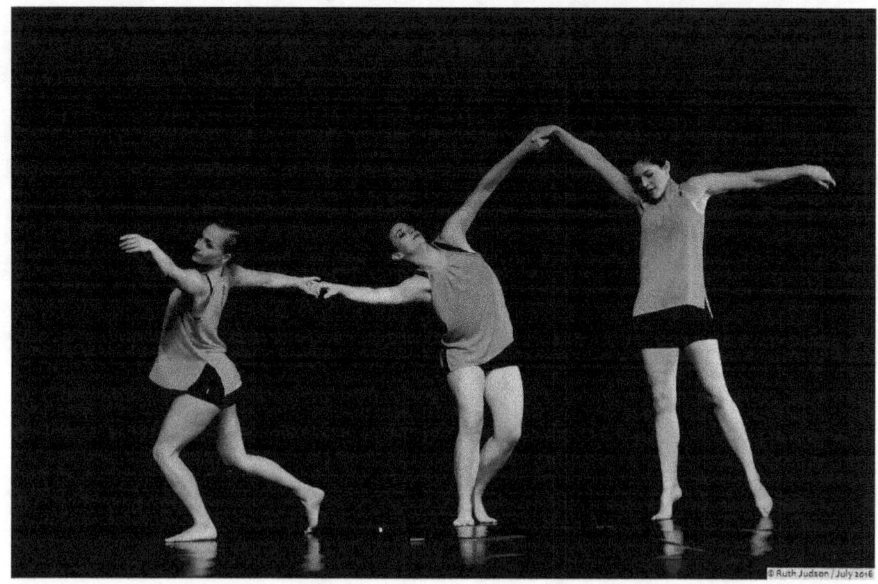

"The Chaos in which we live does not overwhelm us."
Photo credit: Ruth Judson

To forge a bond

One can be overpowered

Two can defend themselves

A cord of three strands is not easily broken

We are not alone

We are not lost

The Chaos in which we live

Does not overwhelm us

The universe has order

We have one another

4 – FRACTALS

The invisible made visible
The mathematics of the eye

Mandlebrot saw
Patterns of chaos
The natural world
He gave them a name
Fractal
Fragmented
Broken
The study of roughness
The study of beauty

Euclid saw
Straight lines, smooth surfaces
A world of cones, spheres, cubes
A world made by men
Mandlebrot saw
Chaos, spontaneity, surprise
A world of coastlines and galaxies
Discovering a New World
Needing a new geometry

Fractals
Occupying
An unfamiliar dimension

Not one dimensional, two, three

But somewhere in between

A small piece of the whole

Infinitely replicating

Infinitely reiterating

The fronds of a fern

The branches of a tree

Those at the base

Predicting the pattern

The rest follow

A cluster of trees

Predicting the pattern

Of the forest

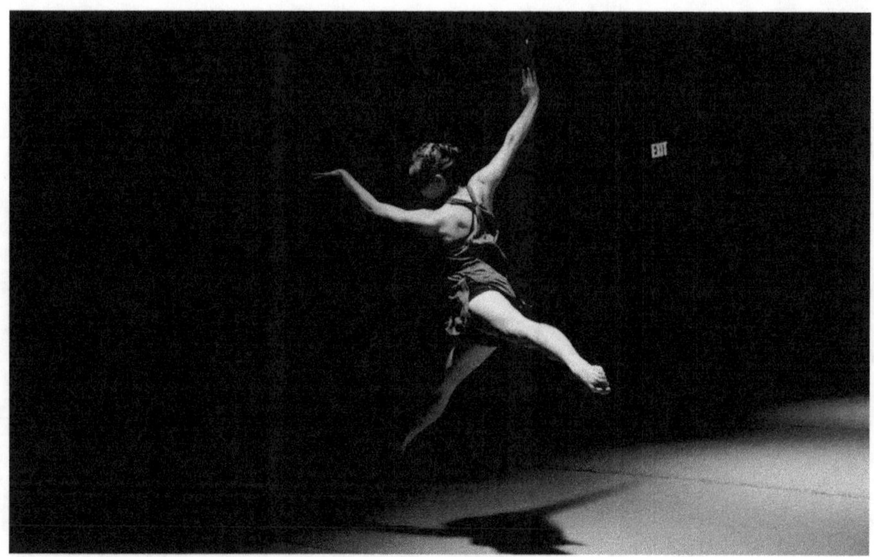

"We choose to depart, dancing instead to Fibonacci's pulse."
Photo credit: Ruth Judson

Exhaling the oxygen
We take into lungs
That bear their shape
Carried away by a network
Of self-same branching
Vessels

We tame the chaos of motion
Into the rhythms of dance
The twos and fours
Of our heartbeats
The rhythms of Euclid

Or we choose to depart
Dancing instead
To Fibonnaci's pulse

0 and 1...1
1 and 1...2
1 and 2...3
2 and 3...5
3 and 5...8
5 and 8...13
8 and 13...21...

5 – SOLO

Most of us see
The rings of the tree
Concentric circles of light and dark
A record of life
Traubeck
Heard music
Trapped in those rings
Gathered their color and texture
With sensors
Found language in algorithm
Extracted musical notes
Captured the nuances
Of
Spruce, ash, oak, maple
It is to their music we dance

They lend their voices to
The music of the spheres
The hum of the sun, the moon
The Earth
Energy made tangible
Through mathematics
Translated into
Music
We join our voices
Our bodies

To theirs

Our collaboration

A dance

The branches of those trees

Replicated in the dancers' bodies

Lungs, eyes, blood, brain

Fractal patterns

Knitting us to the universe

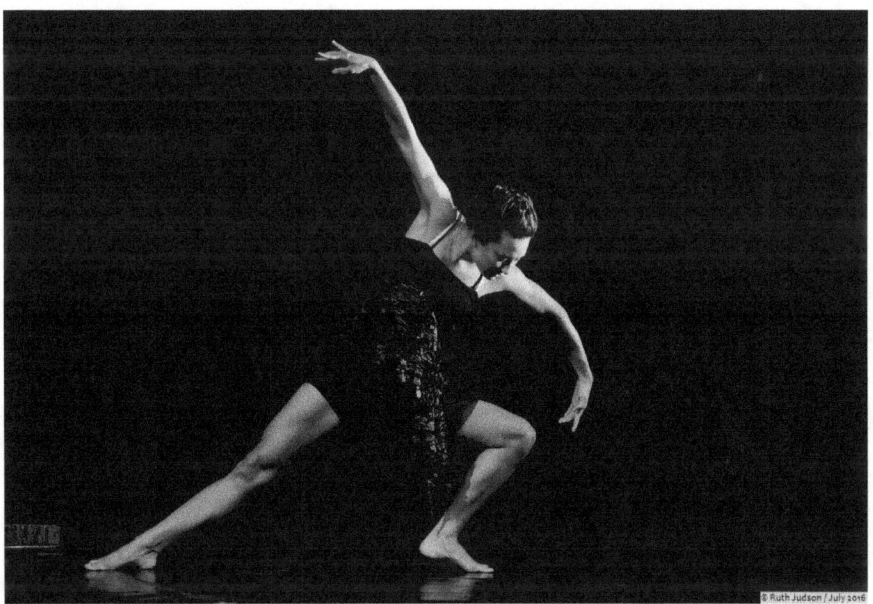

"We reach for the sky and cling to the ground."
Photo credit: Ruth Judson

We dance patterns

We dance paintings

We reach for the sky

And cling to the ground

Art
Seeking order amid
Chaos
Translating it to a language
We all speak

6 – SEA GLASS

Ocean waves
Bearing smaller waves
Carrying them like children
Smaller versions of themselves
Pushing their way onto the shore
Their ebb and flow
Leaving traces of their visit
A fractal pattern on the sand
Over time
A gradual wearing away
A fractal coastline

The sea urchin
An illustration of
Mandelbrot's set
The seahorse
Bears the image of Julia's
A family resemblance
The nautilus
A Fibonacci spiral

Turbulence
The patterns of the
flowing water
Fractal flora
Algae blooms and coral
The landscape of sea grass

Sound
Motion
Always-changing
Ever-present
We are soothed
By its sound
It reminds us to breathe
To draw slow, deep breath
To consider
What lies beneath
Beneath the waves
Beneath the sea
Beneath the surface
Of those we know best
Of those we love

We live in Chaos
Each of our actions
Bearing consequences
For those around us

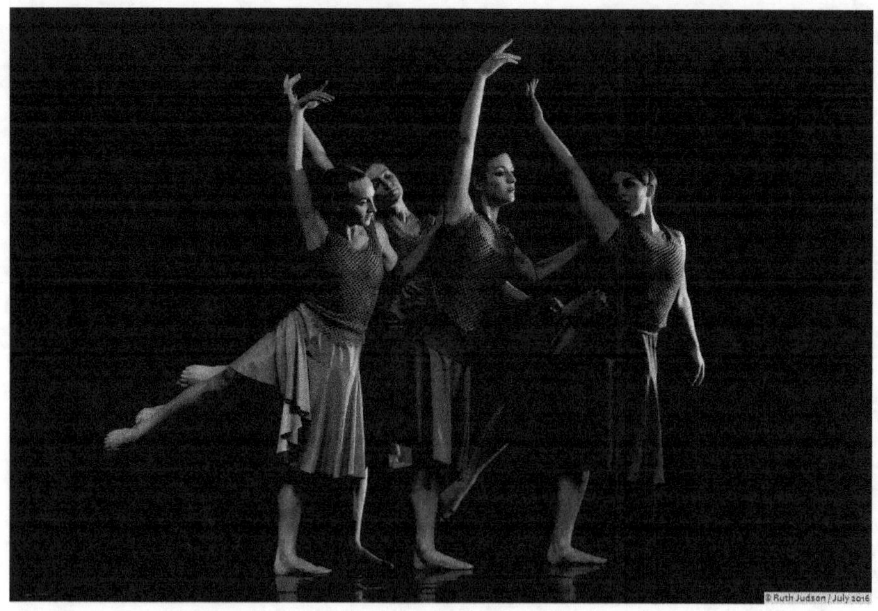

"We strive to restore Order, to make it, to keep it."
Photo credit: Ruth Judson

We strive to restore Order

To make it, to keep it

We sort the world around us

Starting at the surface

We read appearances

What we think we see

Only a clue

To what is hidden

To what lies beneath

The invisible made visible

Our faces, our bodies

Self-similar

Repeating

We are alike

We are one

PROSE

Dotted lines signify complete ideas. The lines between them function as sentences and paragraphs.

1 - INTRODUCTION

GARRETT

1490. Leonardo da Vinci, realizing the work of an ancient architect, making mathematics visible,

ASHLEY

Blending art and science, geometry and human proportion, recognizing the divine,

KIMBERLEY

The length of the arms equal to a person's height,

ASHLEY

From knee to foot, from elbow to fingertip, one quarter of a person's height, a golden ratio,

KIMBERLEY

Evidence of a plan amid the chaos of being human.

GARRETT

2000 years previous, Pythagoras used the circle to represent the spiritual realm — the square, the material world.

KIMBERLEY

da Vinci saw them as one, and if the human form, then so the universe.

ASHLEY

1202. Leonardo Bonacci, realizing the work of ancient India, making mathematics visible,

GARRETT

Studying population, multiplying rabbits, finding a solution in a sequence of numbers.

GARRETT (ALL on sums)

0 and 1…1
1 and 1…2
1 and 2…3
2 and 3…5
3 and 5…8
5 and 8…13
8 and 13…21

GARRETT

Plants innately know to flower this way, to blossom, to branch. Pinecones and pineapples, sunflowers, spiralize into this sequence — knowing no math, knowing only efficiency, knowing how to flourish. The starfish, the nautilus shell, our lungs, our blood vessels — we thrive and survive in these numbers.

ASHLEY

1883. Georg Cantor, realizing the work of one of his contemporaries, making mathematics visible, dropped the middle third of a line, and the middle third of the remaining lines, and the middle third of those, repeating infinitely, the Perfect Set.

KIMBERLEY

1904. Helge von Koch, realizing the work of Georg Cantor, making mathematics visible, devises a curve composed of straight lines, infinitely long yet finite in its area, a pathological shape, a snowflake.

An idea, evolving through time from before 1202…to 1490…1883…1904…

1980.

ASHLEY

Benoit Mandelbrot, realizing the work of Julia and Fatou, exploding the limits

GARRETT

of nature, of art, of music, of architecture, biology, medicine, finance, mathematics,

ALL

making it visible,

GARRETT

giving it a name,

ALL

"fractals."

GARRETT

Patterns of shapes, self-same shapes differing only in size, in scale, repeating, reiterating

ALL

all around us.

GARRETT

Before Mandelbrot,

ASHLEY

before Koch,

KIMBERLEY

before Cantor,

JEREMIAH

before Fibonacci,

GABE

da Vinci,

JEREMIAH

Vitruvius,

GABE

Pythagoras,

ALL

the invisible world made visible.

ASHLEY

We do not see them into being.

GARRETT

They are there.

ALL

They wait to be known.

2 – INCONSCIENT

ALL

We miss what surrounds us, right before our eyes

KIMBERLEY

A world that exists in all its complexity whether we know it, or see it, or acknowledge it.

Inconscient, mindless, distracted, preoccupied — a world in motion – frenetic, chaotic.

We could go in any direction we choose, and yet we move with the crowd, an organism, a fractal.

Rush hour, a woman finds herself seven feet undergrounds suddenly, a sinkhole, alone, helpless, no reply from the hundreds just above.

We miss what surrounds us, right before our eyes.

She felt control a moment ago. Now she sees it for what it is — a comfort, an illusion.

She raises an umbrella. No response. She waits for rescue

We miss what surrounds us, right before our eyes. We don't know to look. We don't stop to notice.

3 – CORD OF THREE STRANDS

KIMBERLEY

Fractals. Their logic, design, attraction is their power. They provide order, sense, safety in a world that looks (on its surface) tumultuous, disordered.

ASHLEY

Pollock understood layering paint, imitating nature, adopting its dynamics.

KIMBERLEY

van Gogh captured the patterns in the turbulence rather than the darkness of the night.

ASHLEY

Hokusai saw the crest of the wave, not its danger; the wings of a bird, not its distance.

KIMBERLEY

We seek a language to make sense from confusion, to forge a bond.

ASHLEY

One can be overpowered,

KIMBERLEY

Two can defend themselves,

BOTH

A cord of three strands is not easily broken.

ASHLEY

We are not alone. We are not lost.

KIMBERLEY

The Chaos in which we live does not overwhelm us. The universe has order.

BOTH

We have one another.

4 – FRACTALS

ALL

The invisible made visible, the mathematics of the eye.

GARRETT

Mandelbrot saw patterns of chaos, the natural world. He gave them a name.

Fractal: fragmented, broken; the study of roughness, the study of beauty.

Euclid saw straight lines, smooth surfaces, a world of cones, spheres, cubes — a world made by men. Mandelbrot saw chaos, spontaneity, surprise — a world of coastlines and galaxies. Discovering a New World, needing a new geometry. [To discover a new world, he needed a new geometry.]

Fractals. Occupying an unfamiliar dimension — not one dimensional, two, three, but somewhere in between, a small piece of the whole, infinitely replicating, infinitely reiterating. The fronds of a fern, the branches of a tree (those at the base predicting the pattern the rest follow), a cluster of trees predicting the pattern of the forest, exhaling the oxygen we take into lungs that bear their shape, carried away by a network of self-same branching vessels.

We tame the chaos of motion into the rhythms of dance: the twos and fours of our heartbeats the rhythms of Euclid; or we choose to depart, dancing instead to Fibonnaci's pulse.

ALL

0 and 1...1

1 and 1...2

1 and 2...3

2 and 3...5

3 and 5...8

5 and 8...13

8 and 13...21...

5 – SOLO

ASHLEY

Most of us see the rings of the tree, concentric circles of light and dark, a record of life. Traubeck heard music trapped in those rings: gathered their color and texture with sensors, found language in algorithm, extracted musical notes, captured the nuances of spruce, ash, oak, maple. It is to their music we dance.

They lend their voices to the music of the spheres: the hum of the sun, the moon, the Earth. Energy made tangible through mathematics, translated into music. We join our voices, our bodies to theirs, our collaboration a dance. The branches of those trees replicated in the dancers' bodies: lungs, eyes, blood, brain. Fractal patterns knitting us to the universe.

We dance patterns. We dance paintings. We reach for the sky and cling to the ground. Art seeking order amid chaos, translating it to a language we all speak.

6 – SEA GLASS

KIMBERLEY

Ocean waves (bearing smaller waves, carrying them like children, smaller versions of themselves) pushing their way onto the shore, their ebb and flow leaving traces of their visit, a fractal pattern on the sand — over time, a gradual wearing away, a fractal coastline.

The sea urchin an illustration of Mandelbrot's set, the seahorse bears the image of Julia's — a family resemblance — the nautilus, a Fibonacci spiral.

Turbulence, the patterns of the flowing water — fractal flora; algae blooms and coral — the landscape of sea grass.

ASHLEY

Sound, motion, always-changing, ever-present. We are soothed by its sound.

It reminds us to breathe, to draw slow, deep breath. [It reminds us] to consider what lies beneath; beneath the waves, beneath the sea, beneath the surface, of those we know best, of those we love.

GARRETT

We live in Chaos, each of our actions bearing consequences for those around us. We strive to restore Order, to make it, to keep it.

JEREMIAH

We sort the world around us, starting at the surface.

GABE

We read appearances; what we think we see only a clue to what is hidden, to what lies beneath.

ALL

[What lies beneath is] The invisible made visible.

GABE

Our faces, our bodies

JEREMIAH

Self-similar

GARRETT

Repeating

ASHLEY

We are alike.

ALL

We are one.

THE SCRIPT (ANNOTATED)

1 - INTRODUCTION

Darkness.

Spotlight. One actor stands behind another (JEREMIAH and GABE) modeling the Vitruvian Man.

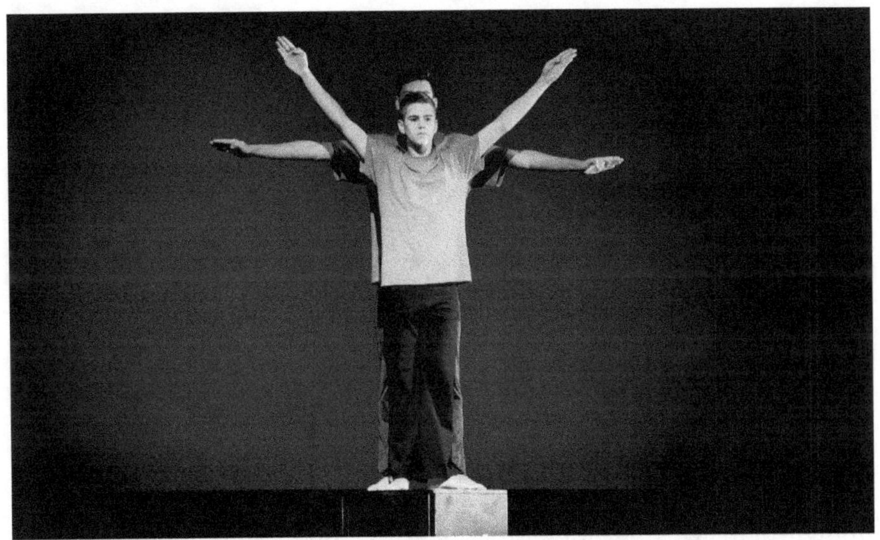

Vitruvian Man
Photo credit: Ruth Judson

> Vitruvian Man, so called because da Vinci modeled it on the earlier work of Vitruvius (Marcus Vitruvius Pollio, born 80-70 BCE, died after 15 BCE)

GARRETT

1490
Leonardo da Vinci
Realizing the work
Of an ancient architect
Making mathematics visible

ASHLEY

Blending art and science
Geometry and human proportion
Recognizing the divine

(Jeremiah and Gabe illustrate the following)

KIMBERLEY

The length of the arms equal to a person's height

ASHLEY

From knee to foot, from elbow to fingertip
One quarter of a person's height
A golden ratio

> Golden ratio is a key concept and ties the work of da Vinci not only to Vitruvius but forward in time to Fibonacci, through history, encompassing all the future work and discovery around fractals.

KIMBERLEY

Evidence of a plan

Amid the chaos of being human

Chaos theory and fractals

Great working definition on the Fractal Foundation website:

Chaos is the science of surprises, of the nonlinear and the unpredictable. It teaches us to expect the unexpected. While most traditional science deals with supposedly predictable phenomena like gravity, electricity, or chemical reactions, Chaos Theory deals with nonlinear things that are effectively impossible to predict or control, like turbulence, weather, the stock market, our brain states, and so on. These phenomena are often described by fractal mathematics, which captures the infinite complexity of nature.

Vitruvian Man

https://leonardodavinci.stanford.edu/submissions/clabaugh/history/leonardo.html

https://www.bl.uk/learning/cult/bodies/vitruvius/proportion.html

These articles have images that show the difference in da Vinci's understanding of proportion in human anatomy from Vitruvius' understanding.

All of these stanzas recognize that without the work of those who came before, the evolution of ideas is not possible. Each innovator is a genius in his own right, and the ones who follow stand on the shoulders of those who preceded them.

Enrico Giaccherini identifies this as a type of collaboration, one person building on the work on another.

GARRETT

2000 years previous

Pythagoras

Used the circle to represent the spiritual realm,

The square, the material world

> "In all cultures with an architectural history, the square and the cube were assigned to the material or the element "earth" and therefore the number 4 . . . Vitruvius considers the number 4 to be man's number since, with outstretched arms, his width equals his height, thus marking the height and width of an ideal square . . .As an infinite line, the circle may symbolize anything infinite: time, eternity, infinity. The circle symbolizes the periodicity of human life and the laws of nature."
>
> *Architecture and Mathematics from Antiquity to the Future: Volume One: Antiquity to the 1500s,* Kim Williams and Michael J. Ostwald (2015; Basel, Switzerland; Birkhäuser Verlag) 82-83.

KIMBERLEY

da Vinci

Saw them as one

And if the human form

Then so the universe

(All actors at the mic. They stand in a horizontal line.)

ASHLEY

1202

Leonardo Bonacci

Realizing the work

Of ancient India

Making mathematics visible

> Bonacci's *Liber Abaci* was the first Western work to bring Hindu-Arabic numerals and place value into use. The Fibonacci series is present in the work of 6th c. Indian mathematicians.

GARRETT

Studying population

Multiplying rabbits

Finding a solution

In a sequence of numbers

> Fibonacci was interested in theoretical population growth, specifically the question of how many rabbits would result from *n* breeding sessions following a set of idealized rules. The solution was the now famous Fibonacci series, found throughout the natural world. Mandelbrot later used the M-Set as a way to examine not only population growth but financial markets and other areas of exponential growth and decline.
>
> An internet search of "Fibonacci in nature" or "golden ratio in nature" yields a wealth of information and illustrations.

(GARRETT speaks the sequence at the mic. The others model the sequence, speaking on the sums.)

GARRETT

0 and 1…1

1 and 1…2

1 and 2…3

2 and 3…5

3 and 5…8

5 and 8…13

8 and 13…21

(They illustrate the Fibonacci spiral as GARRETT continues.)

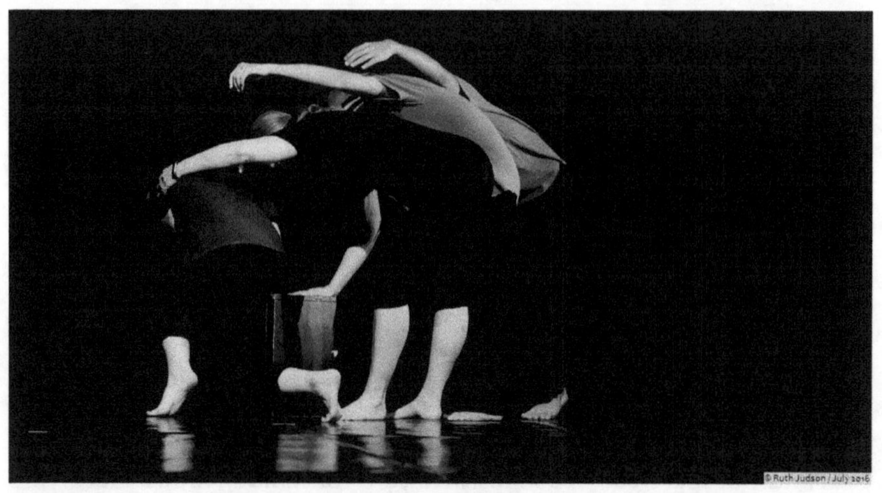

The Cast as a Fibonacci spiral
Photo credit: Ruth Judson

GARRETT

Plants innately know

To flower this way

To blossom

To branch

Pinecones and pineapples
Sunflowers
Spiralize into this sequence

Knowing no math
Knowing only efficiency
Knowing how to
Flourish

The starfish, the nautilus shell
Our lungs, our blood vessels
We thrive and survive in these numbers

Our lungs and our circulatory systems follow branching patterns, which are fractal in nature; reiterating, self-similar patterns.

(ASHLEY at the mic. The rest model the Cantor Set as the following is spoken.)

ASHLEY

1883
Georg Cantor
Realizing the work
Of one of his contemporaries
Making mathematics visible

Dropped the middle third of a line
And the middle third of the remaining lines

And the middle third of those

Repeating

Infinitely

The Perfect Set

Henry John Stephen Smith actually discovered the mathematics that became known as the Cantor Set, but he died in 1883. Cantor published the idea, introducing it to the public in a much broader sense than the expression of it that was associated with Smith alone.

A perfect set is a closed set with no isolated points, a set that lacks density.

(KIMBERLEY at the mic, ASHLEY joins the others. They model the shape of the first several iterations of the Koch snowflake as the following is spoken.)

KIMBERLEY

1904

Helge von Koch

Realizing the work

Of Georg Cantor

Making mathematics visible

Devises a curve

Composed of straight lines

Infinitely long

Yet finite in its area

A pathological shape

A snowflake

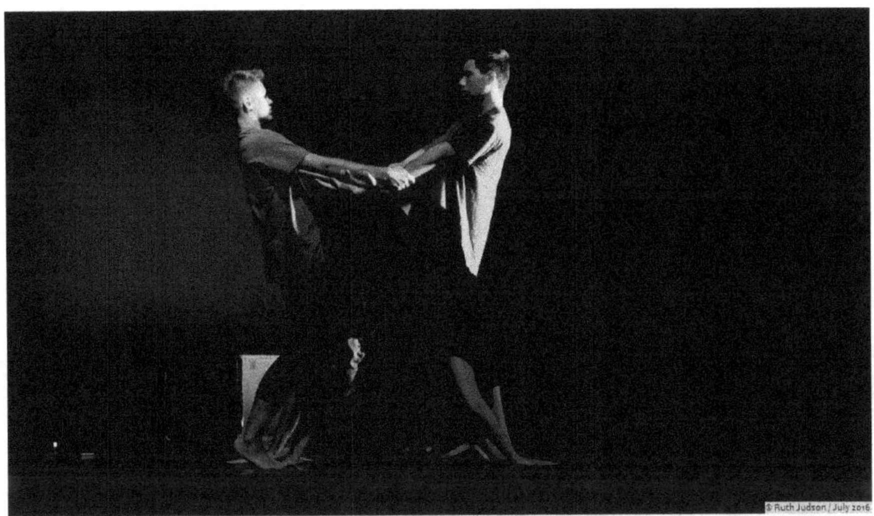

The Cast as a Koch snowflake
Photo credit: Ruth Judson

Pathological shapes are measured with regard to their convexity.

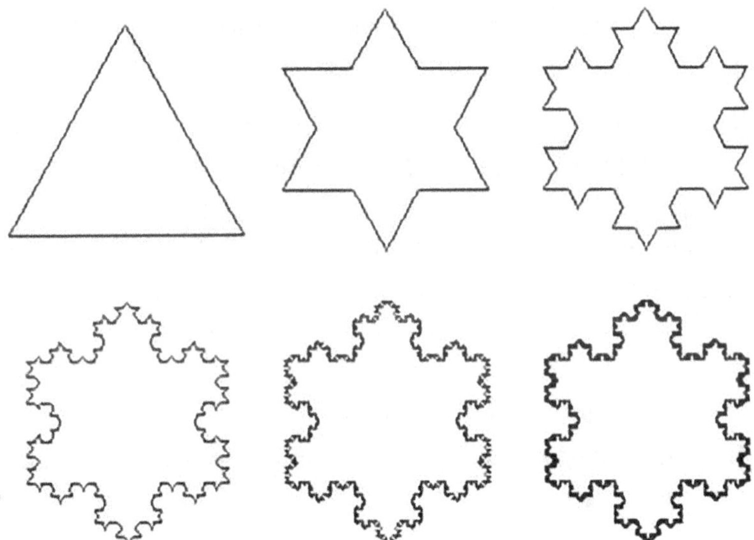

Koch curve to Koch snowflake, progression

Contemporary science has and continues to build on this work, extending it to new applications.

Mandelbrot applied the underlying concept of the Koch curve in seeking to measure the English coastline. He recognized that the smaller the measure he used, the greater would be his accuracy. He wanted to measure it in its roughness, not in its length. This led him closer toward his discovery of fractal geometry, the notion of needing a new geometry to understand the natural world, and the notion that this would require a new understanding of dimensionality — fractals exist between the third and fourth dimension. His first published study on coastlines was in 1967; he published his landmark text, 'The Fractal Nature of Geometry' in 1975.

Nathan Cohen used the concept of the Koch curve to create a smaller antenna with a wider range of frequency. Its smaller size and cheaper cost enable it to meet complex technological needs. This is the type of antenna now used in cell phones, among other electronics. He began the conceptual work underlying this technology is 1988, and first published his results in 1995.

Branching patterns are an expression of both the Fibonacci spiral and the Cantor Set. In 1999, West, Brown, and Endquist studied branching patterns in the rain forest in Costa Rica to better understand energy use and CO_2 levels. They discovered that not only trees are fractal in the way they establish a branching pattern from the trunk to the smallest twig, but that a whole forest follows a given pattern. Based on this concept, the medical world is able to identify disruptions in a patient's circulatory system; where the branching pattern is disrupted, cancer cells have set up an independent system.

An idea

Evolving through time

From before 1202…to 1490…1883…1904…

(ALL return to the mic)

1980

The idea of fractals evolved through time from before Bonacci…to da Vinci…to Cantor…to Koch…to Mandelbrot…and beyond.

ASHLEY

Benoit Mandelbrot

Realizing the work

Of Julia and Fatou

The mathematicians

Of his youth

Exploding the limits

Relationship of the Julia Set to the M-Set

Mandelbrot studied the work of Gaston Julia and Pierre Fatou, responsible in their day for the mathematical discovery of complementary sets – the Julia set was described as laces, the Fatou set as dusts.

Mandelbrot saw nothing in their work to which he could add, so he put it aside; but he kept it in mind. Decades later as computer technology enabled him to explore more complex mathematical questions, he asked this: Because each Julia set J_c is either connected or a dust, can we draw a map of the c for which Jc is connected? The result of this question was the Mandelbrot set, a roadmap giving the locations of all the connected Julia sets.

This discovery blew the world of fractal geometry wide open.

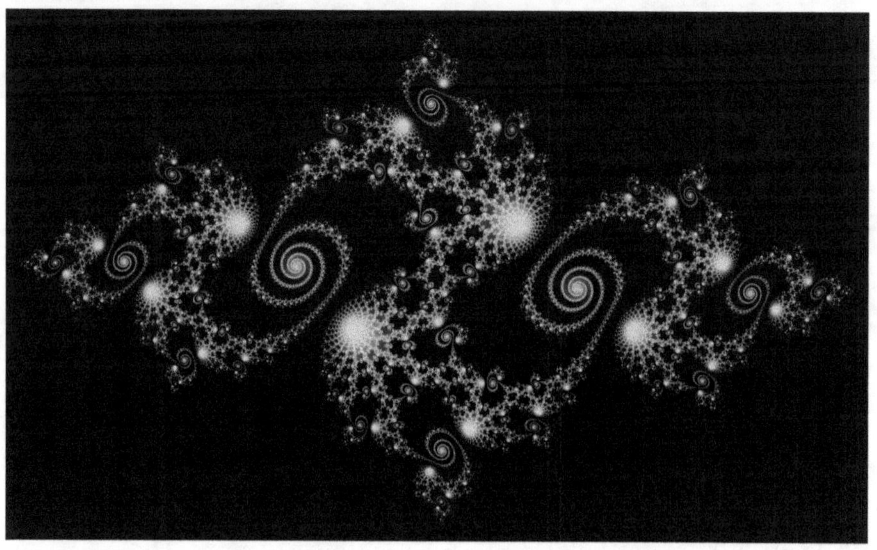

Julia Set, illustrated

GARRETT

Of nature

Of art

Of music

Of architecture

Biology

Medicine

Finance

Mathematics

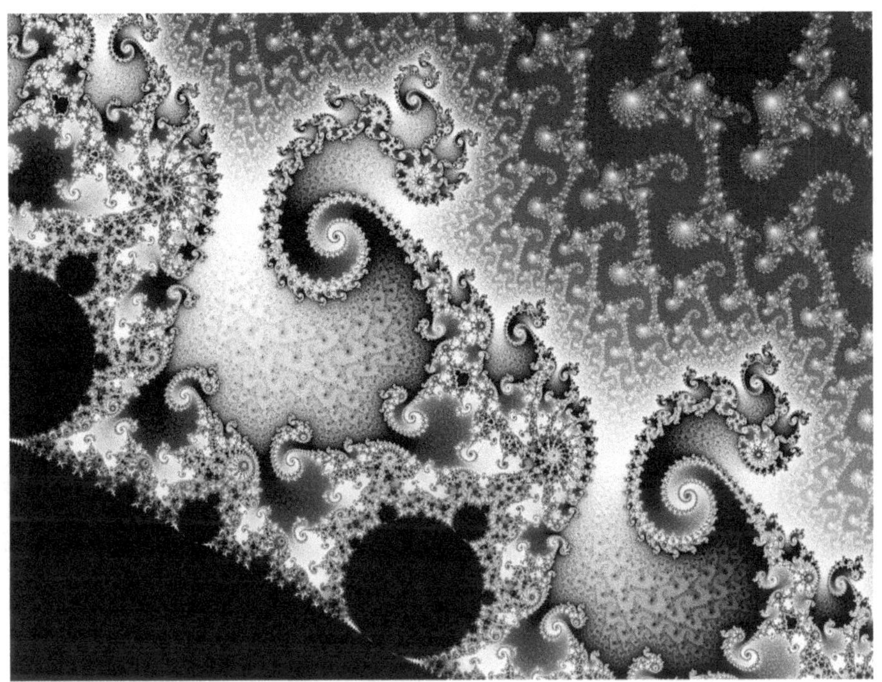

Mandlebrot set, illustrated

ALL

Making it visible

GARRETT

Giving it a name

ALL

Fractals

GARRETT

Patterns of shapes
Self-same shapes

Differing only in size

In scale

Repeating

Reiterating

ALL

All around us

> The three fundamental properties of fractals are self-similarity, repeated iteration, and non-integer dimension.

GARRETT

Before Mandelbrot

ASHLEY

Before Koch

KIMBERLEY

Before Cantor

JEREMIAH

Before Fibonacci

GABE

da Vinci

JEREMIAH

Vitruvius

GABE

Pythagoras

ALL

The invisible world made visible

ASHLEY

We do not see them into being

GARRETT

They are there

ALL

They wait to be known

2 – INCONSCIENT

ALL

We miss what surrounds us
Right before our eyes

KIMBERLEY

A world that exists
In all its complexity
Whether we know it
Or see it
Or acknowledge it

Inconscient
Mindless
Distracted
Preoccupied
A world in motion
Frenetic

Chaotic

We could go in any direction
we choose
And yet we move with the crowd
An organism
A fractal

Crowd movement and dynamics translate into fractal shapes and patterns. The body of scholarly work around this lends insight into diverse applications including city planning, crowd control, and epidemiology.

Rush hour
A woman finds herself
Seven feet underground
Suddenly
A sinkhole
Alone
Helpless
No reply
From the hundreds
Just above

She raises an umbrella
No response

She waits for rescue

This event actually occurred and is described in Heather Zempel's 2014 book, *Amazed and Confused*. On a typical Friday evening walk from her Senate office to her apartment on Capitol Hill in Washington, D.C., Zempel reports that she did not step into the hole; the ground literally opened up and swallowed her. It was raining, and she had an umbrella with her, which she tried to use to gain the attention of someone at street level, to no avail. She was stranded and alone in the middle of a busy city in the middle of rush hour.

We miss what surrounds us

Right before our eyes

We don't know to look

We don't stop to notice

3 – CORD OF THREE STRANDS

KIMBERLEY

Fractals

Their logic, design

Attraction

Is their power

A mathematical attractor is a set of numerical values toward which a system tends to evolve. Attractors are called "strange attractors" when they have a fractal structure. Mandelbrot called them "fractal attractors" because they are the most common ones found in nature, not strange at all.

They provide

Order, sense

Safety

In a world that looks

On its surface

Tumultuous, disordered

"While most traditional science deals with supposedly predictable phenomena like gravity, electricity, or chemical reactions, Chaos Theory deals with nonlinear things that are effectively impossible to predict or control, like turbulence, weather, the stock market, our brain states, and so on. These phenomena are often described by fractal mathematics, which captures the infinite complexity of nature. Many natural objects exhibit fractal properties, including landscapes, clouds, trees, organs, rivers, etc., and many of the systems in which we live exhibit complex, chaotic behavior." (www.fractalfoundation.org)

Chaos is not simply disorder. Chaos Theory explores the transitions between order and disorder.

ASHLEY

Pollock understood

Layering paint

Imitating nature

Adopting its dynamics

Pollock captured an aesthetic dimension in his work that physicist and art historian Richard Taylor later studied, analyzed, and identified as a product of both chaos theory and fractal geometry.

Taylor once remarked, "If someone asked, 'Can I have nature put into a piece of canvas?' the best example there has ever been of that is Pollock's *Number 14*. Pollock painted in fractal dimension because he was closely attuned to the natural world." Experts such as Taylor can identify forgeries because they lack fractal dimension.

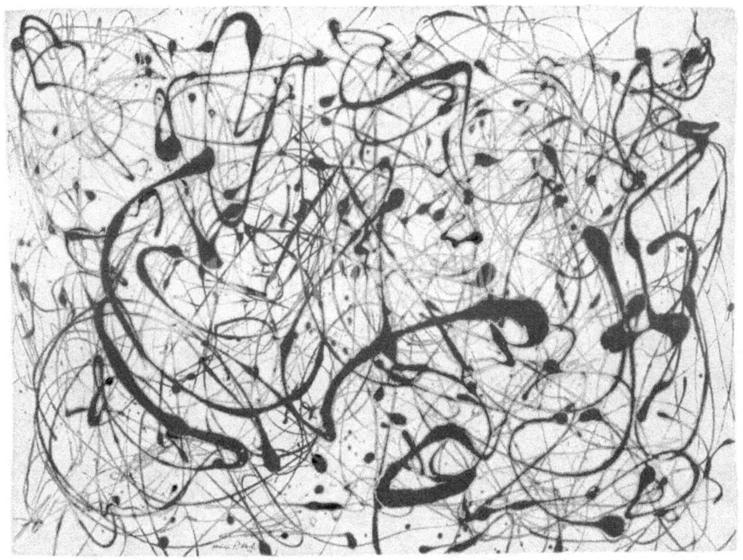

Jackson Pollock, "Number 14"

KIMBERLEY

van Gogh captured

The patterns in the turbulence

Rather than the

Darkness of the night

Turbulence is fractal in nature. During the period of his life when he experienced prolonged psychotic agitation, van Gogh captured turbulence in his paintings in ways that illustrate the mathematical structure of turbulent flow.

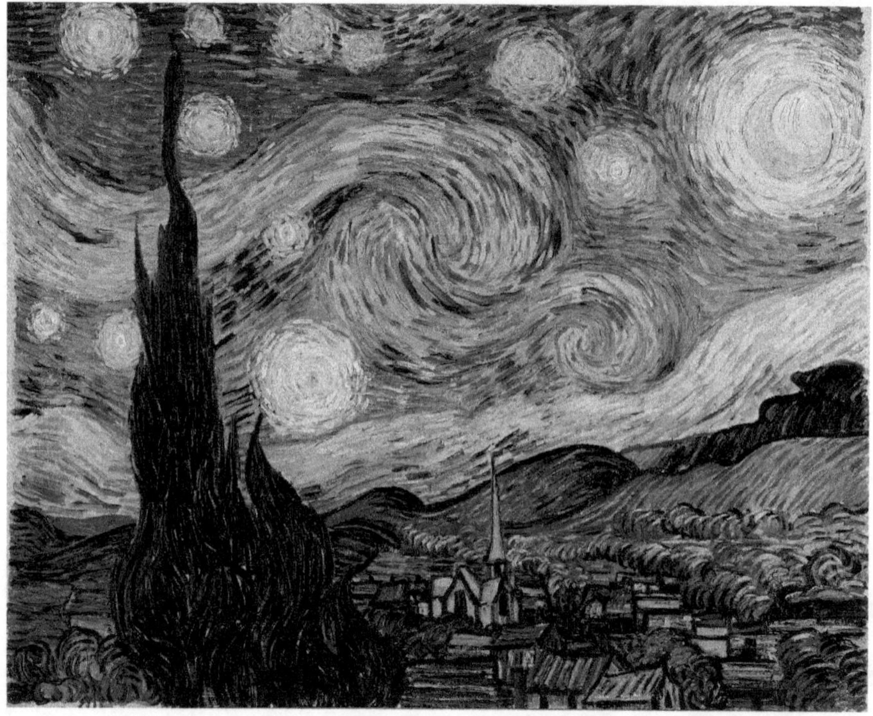

Vincent van Gogh, "The Starry Night"

ASHLEY

Hokusai saw

The crest of the wave

Not its danger

The wings of a bird

Not its distance

Hokusai had no mathematical training but had an innate understanding of fractal structure. The most famous example of this is his woodblock "The Great Wave Off Kanagawa," created sometime between 1829 and 1833. In particular, he captures the self-similarity of the breaking waves. In other works, he illustrated the fractal nature of trees, cloud formations, and other elements of the natural world.

One analysis observes that in his "Fuji From the Seashore," the seaweed pattern closely resembles a filled-in Julia Set.

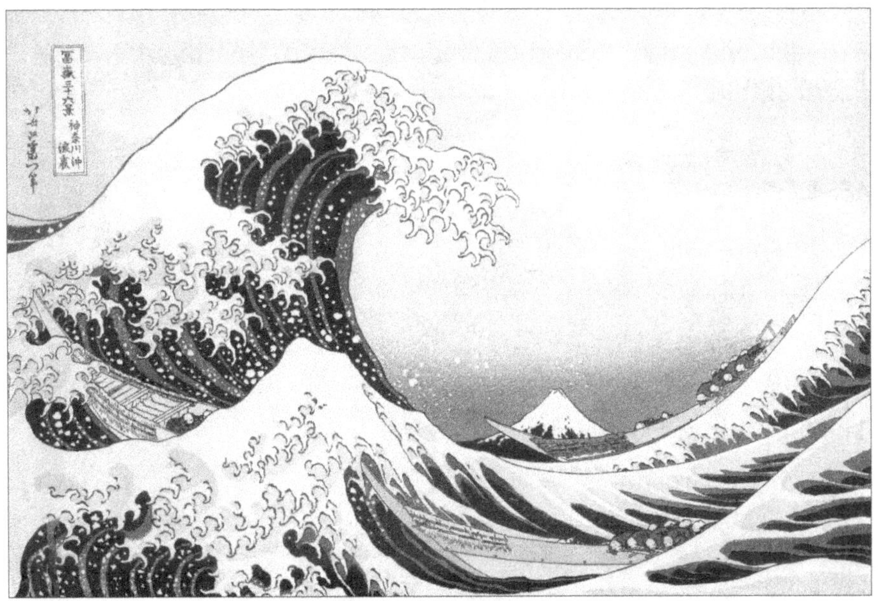

Hokusai, "The Great Wave off Kanagawa"

KIMBERLEY

We seek a language

To make sense from confusion

To forge a bond

ASHLEY

One can be overpowered

KIMBERLEY

Two can defend themselves

BOTH

A cord of three strands is not easily broken

> Ecclesiates 4:12 (NIV translation)
>
> Though one may be overpowered, two can defend themselves. A cord of three strands is not quickly broken.

ASHLEY

We are not alone
We are not lost

KIMBERLEY

The Chaos in which we live
Does not overwhelm us
The universe has order

> The natural world looks arbitrary but is exquisitely ordered, to the smallest detail.

BOTH

We have one another

4 – FRACTALS

ALL

The invisible made visible

The mathematics of the eye

GARRETT

Mandlebrot saw

Patterns of chaos

The natural world

He gave them a name

Fractal

Fragmented

Broken

The study of roughness

The study of beauty

Euclid saw

Straight lines, smooth surfaces

A world of cones, spheres, cubes

A world made by men

Mandlebrot saw

Chaos, spontaneity, surprise

A world of coastlines and galaxies

Discovering a New World

Needing a new geometry

The coastline paradox is the counterintuitive observation that the coastline of a landmass does not have a well-defined length. This results from the fractal-like properties of coastlines. The first recorded observation of this phenomenon was by Lewis Fry Richardson. Benoit Mandelbrot expanded it.

Mandelbrot published *How Long Is the Coast of Britain? Statistical Self-Similarity and Fractional Dimension* in the journal *Science* in 1967. In this paper, Mandelbrot discusses self-similar curves that have Hausdorff dimension between 1 and 2. These curves are examples of fractals, although Mandelbrot does not use this term in the paper; he did not coin it until 1975. The paper is one of Mandelbrot's first publications on the topic of fractals.

Epistemology is the branch of philosophy concerned with the theory of knowledge. We each have different ways of seeing and ways of knowing, a different lens with which we encounter and make sense of the world around us. This is one of the many reasons we need one another. We need the piece each of us holds to gain a more complete view of the world we share.

Fractals

Occupying

An unfamiliar dimension

Not one dimensional, two, three

But somewhere in between

A small piece of the whole

Infinitely replicating

Infinitely reiterating

The fronds of a fern

The branches of a tree

Those at the base

Predicting the pattern

The rest follow

A cluster of trees

Predicting the pattern

Of the forest

Exhaling the oxygen

We take into lungs

That bear their shape

Carried away by a network

Of self-same branching

Vessels

A reference to West, Brown and Enquist's work on C02 emissions in the rain forest.

The Cantor Set is the basis of understanding branching systems in fractal terms.

We tame the chaos of motion

Into the rhythms of dance

The twos and fours

Of our heartbeats

The rhythms of Euclid

Dancer and choreographer Catherine Turocy published on fractals in dance in the Winter 2012 issue of *Early Music America*. She observes the fractal patterns of the movement in Baroque dance, specifically elements such as da Vinci's circle-in-a-square as used in the Vitruvian Man, Fibonacci spirals, and the Golden Ratio. She notes the self-similarity and re-iteration in both the patterns and movement of the dance.

Or we choose to depart

Dancing instead

To Fibonnaci's pulse

> And while our pulse, our heartbeat, is typically a steady 1-2, 1-2, the circulatory system itself is fractal, a branching system – as is the visual representation from an EKG.
>
> The variation in branching patterns of the circulatory system can be used to distinguish normal patients from those who have experienced heart failure.

ALL

0 and 1…1

1 and 1…2

1 and 2…3

2 and 3…5

3 and 5…8

5 and 8…13

8 and 13…21…

> Meredith Barnes' choreography for *Fractals* is set on Fibonacci counts, not the meter of the music on which she set the piece.

5– SOLO

ASHLEY

Most of us see

The rings of the tree

Concentric circles of light and dark

A record of life

Traubeck

Heard music

Trapped in those rings

Gathered their color and texture

With sensors

Found language in algorithm

Extracted musical notes

Captured the nuances

Of

Spruce, ash, oak, maple

It is to their music we dance

Bartholomäus Traubeck (b. 1987) developed laser technology that reads tree rings and translates them into music. It analyzes the rings for strength, thickness, and rate of growth. His recording *Years*, released in 2012, features eight compositions made from Austrian trees: spruce, ash, oak, maple, alder, walnut, and two different beech trees.

Meredith Barnes set the beginning of Darian Iida's *Solo* on Traubeck's *Picea* (Spruce) recording.

They lend their voices to

The music of the spheres

The hum of the sun, the moon

The Earth

Energy made tangible

Through mathematics

Translated into

Music

Musica universalis (literally Universal Music, also called Music of the Spheres or Harmony of the Spheres) is an ancient philosophical concept that regards proportions in the movements of celestial bodies—the Sun, Moon, and planets—as a form of music. This music is not usually thought to be literally audible, but a harmonic, mathematical, or religious concept.

We join our voices
Our bodies
To theirs
Our collaboration
A dance

We breathe their oxygen, they use our CO_2.

The branches of those trees
Replicated in the dancers' bodies
Lungs, eyes, blood, brain

These components of human anatomy are all fractal in nature.

Fractal patterns
Knitting us to the universe

We dance patterns
We dance paintings
We reach for the sky
And cling to the ground

Dance is rooted in the concept of opposition, energy moving in opposite directions to establish balance. It keeps the dancer grounded, in contact with the Earth.

Author Pat Conroy described the same phenomenon this way in his 1986 novel, *The Prince of Tides*:

"The sun, red and enormous, began to sink into the western sky and simultaneously, the moon began to rise on the other side of the river with its own glorious shade of red, coming up out of the trees like a russet firebird. The sun and the moon seemed to acknowledge each other, and they moved in both apposition and concordance in a breathtaking dance of light across the oaks and palms."

This is the intersection of the natural world and the means we use to express our relationship to it and our understanding of it – writing, painting, music, dance, theater, science, mathematics.

Art

Seeking order amid

Chaos

Translating it to a language

We all speak

6 – SEA GLASS

KIMBERLEY

Ocean waves

Bearing smaller waves

Carrying them like children

Smaller versions of themselves

Pushing their way onto the shore

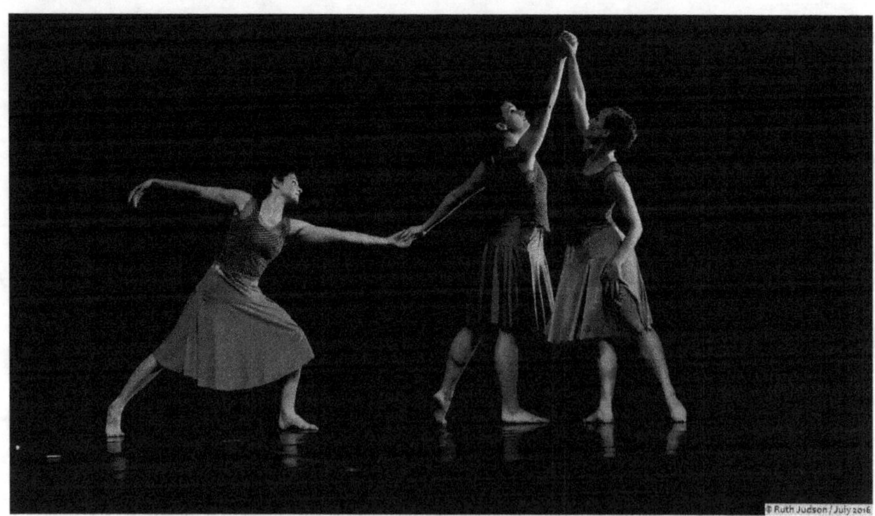

Sea Glass
Photo Credit: Ruth Judson

Their ebb and flow

Leaving traces of their visit

A fractal pattern on the sand

Over time

A gradual wearing away

A fractal coastline

This is a natural phenomenon, the world insisting on fractal structure, the waves not only fractal in themselves but wearing the coastline into fractal shape and dimension.

This is also a reference to Hokusai's fractals waves, van Gogh's turbulence.

The sea urchin

An illustration of

Mandelbrot's set

The seahorse
Bears the image of Julia's
A family resemblance
The nautilus
A Fibonacci spiral
Turbulence
The patterns of the
flowing water
Fractal flora
Algae blooms and coral
The landscape of sea grass

ASHLEY

Sound
Motion
Always-changing
Ever-present
We are soothed
By its sound
It reminds us to breathe
To draw slow, deep breath
To consider
What lies beneath
Beneath the waves
Beneath the sea
Beneath the surface
Of those we know best
Of those we love

GARRETT

We live in Chaos

Each of our actions

Bearing consequences

For those around us

We strive to restore Order

To make it, to keep it

JEREMIAH

We sort the world around us

Starting at the surface

GABE

We read appearances

What we think we see

Only a clue

To what is hidden

To what lies beneath

ALL

The invisible made visible

GABE

Our faces, our bodies

JEREMIAH

Self-similar

GARRETT

Repeating

ASHLEY

We are alike

ALL

We are one

CHAPTER 4

PRODUCTION

Meredith had already applied and been accepted for the 2016 Capital Fringe Festival by the time I became involved in March. At the time she had about half the dance program completed and the other half underway, and a core concept — the production would be in front of an audience by the beginning of July.

I spent March researching and April writing while she continued to develop the dance pieces. We auditioned actors in early May and went into rehearsal just before Memorial Day weekend.

By late June we needed four minutes of material for a preview performance at the Logan Fringe Arts Space in southeast Washington D.C. We had to be ready to tech by the first week in July. It was an incredibly compressed schedule, and we were working with a festival organization known for its disorganization. We had our work cut out.

We were assigned the Elstad Auditorium at Gallaudet University, which carries with it the requirement to provide closed captioning or a sign-language interpreter or both. They provided the equipment needed for closed captioning, so that proved a simple accommodation. Bailey Vincent, a member of DanceArtTheater, is Deaf and was instrumental in helping us to communicate with our on-site technical director, Jacob Fisher. She also helped us to layer some sign language into the dance pieces. Should we find an opportunity to re-mount the show, we would add this to the spoken segments of the performance as well. As it was, the actors were learning text that was evolving as the show developed and learning both movement and dance, so they were at capacity for our twice-weekly rehearsal schedule.

The location was exquisite, a beautiful theater on a beautiful campus, but the nearby highway construction and the heavy volume of traffic typical to Washington D.C. provided another challenge. It was difficult for our cast and staff to arrive at the theater on time, and difficult for our patrons. The Festival schedule is, of necessity, absolute; 15 minutes to load-in and strike, and a running time determined at the time of one's application. Ours was 50 minutes.

The cast and dancers warmed up outside the theater loading dock as we waited to be admitted to the theater space and dodged the incoming cast as we broke down the simple set, props, and equipment following each performance. On one occasion, multiple accidents on the Beltway and outside Union Station (in proximity to the theater) made most of us late for our one-hour pre-show call. At curtain we were missing one actor and one technician as well as many ticket holders, and the Festival graciously moved our curtain time by 15 minutes.

Despite the challenges, the performance was a resounding success. We were reviewed favorably, our audiences were enthusiastic and receptive, and we received a *Best in Fringe* designation from the Festival critics, which drew audience beyond our base and acknowledged our artistic achievement. There were several requests for a copy of the script, which I provided at the time to teachers and mathematicians who wanted the opportunity to consider the work in more depth. These requests were part of the impetus to publish the work, so that others might use it as a model for this genre of theater, and as a means to consider the intersection of academic thought and art as a multidisciplinary approach. This is discussed in more detail in Chapter 5, ***Applications.***

THE COMPANY (DanceArtTheater)

Meredith Barnes, founder and artistic director

Megan Caputo

Ashley Dobrogosz

Madison Horwitz

Darian Iida

Alex Miegal

Erin Ratliff

Jessi Shull

Bailey Vincent

THE CAST

Gabriel Cetron

Kimberley Cetron

Jeremiah Lanoue-Chapman

Gerrett Milich

Ashley Zielinski

THE STAFF

Eryn Barnes, stagehand and closed captioning

Troy Barnes, stagehand

Michael Farish, lighting

Andrea Heininge, stage manager and sound

Jennifer Noda, costume assistant

Jacob Fisher, technical director, Gallaudet Theater Arts

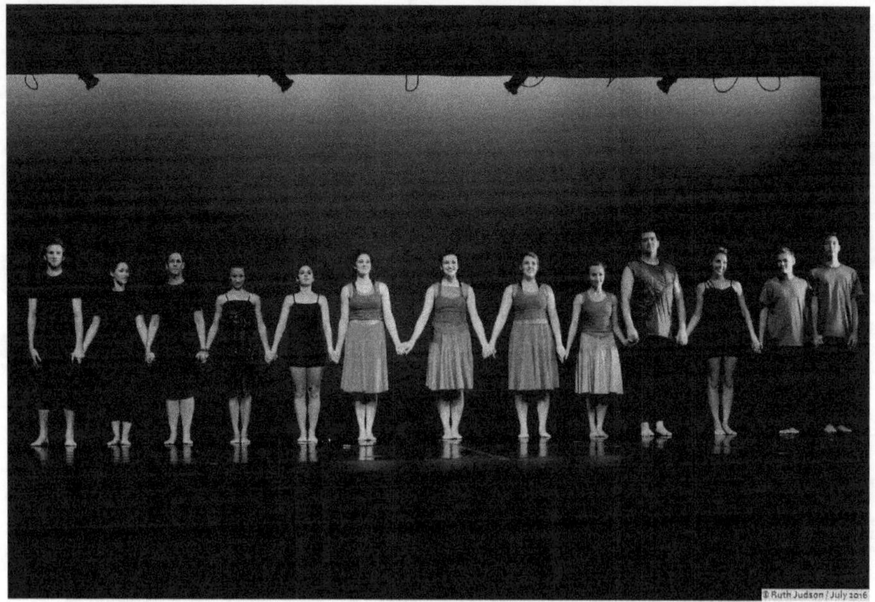

Fractals, opening night curtain call
Photo credit: Ruth Judson

CHAPTER 5

APPLICATIONS

There are three primary audiences who I intend to benefit from the material in this book, from the model of this type of artistic endeavor, and from the potential for its use in educational settings. They are: those involved in theater and dance, professionally and otherwise; writers and writing educators; and educators, both those in arts education and those who seek to mine the potential of the arts for the exploration and mastery of academic subject matter.

THEATER DANCE AND DANCE THEATER

Theater Dance: History and Genre

When we began to conceptualize *Fractals*, I was thinking primarily about Shields/McDonald's *Stay* – not as a model necessarily, but in terms of the potential it exhibited for actors and dancers to collaborate and enter one another's worlds. This led me to wonder what other works might provide guidance or inspiration, and where we might be situated in terms of theater history and genre. I soon realized that this was a project in itself. I could find no one place where someone had considered collaborations between actors and dancers in which each was expected to do the work of the other.

I am a big fan of hive mind, and fortunate that my friends and colleagues are rich resources. They got me started on a list of shows that, while, not exhaustive, is a good representation of both theater history and genre with regard to theater/dance collaborations.

The list grew. Those who read and consider it will have additions, I am sure. I came to consider the list in terms of three different categories: **traditional book musicals** that advanced dance as an art form and/or depended on dance for content; **Broadway performances presented in concert format** that rely primarily on music and dance; and **outliers**, shows which are best considered in and of themselves, shows which approach the ways actors and dancers express themselves and relate to one another in unique capacities.

Traditional Book Musicals

Shuffle Along (1921/1933/1952/2016 adaptation)

No, No, Nanette (1925/1971)

On Your Toes (1936/1954/1983)

Lady in The Dark (1941)

Oklahoma! (1943/1951/1979/2002)

On The Town (1944/1971/1998/2014)

Carousel (1945/1949, 1994/2017)

West Side Story (1957/1960/1980/2009)

Sweet Charity (1966/1986/2005)

Pippin (1972/2013)

A Chorus Line (1975/2006)

My One and Only (1985)

Crazy for You (1992)

Chicago (1975/1996)

The Lion King (1997)

Billy Elliott (2008)

Fela! (2009/2012)

Little Dancer (2014)

An American in Paris (2015)

Broadway Concert Musicals

Dancin' (1978) revue

Cats (1982/2016) musical

Stomp (1991) off-Broadway theatrical show, music and movement

Bring in 'da Noise, Bring in 'da Funk (1996) revue

Fosse (1999) revue

Swing! (1999) musical, no dialogue

Movin' Out (2002) jukebox musical

Burn the Floor (2009) dance concert

Come Fly Away (2010) revue

On Your Feet! (2015) jukebox musical

Outliers

Contact (2000)

Synetic Theater (2001 to present)

Stay (2011)

Cagney (2016)

Paramour (2016)

Traditional Book Musicals: Annotated

Shuffle Along (1921/1933/1952/2016 adaptation)

> Music and lyrics by Noble Sissie and Eubie Blake, book by Flournoy Miller and Aubrey Lyles; 2016 adaptation entitled

Shuffle Along, or the *Making of the Musical Sensation of 1921 and All That Followed*, book by George C. Wolfe.

Long running musical which drew crowds with its jazz music and chorus of professional dancers (16-girl chorus line). Adaptation was the reunion of Wolfe and choreographer Savion Glover, who had previously collaborated on *Bring in 'da Noise, Bring in 'da Funk*.

No, No, Nanette (1925/1971)

Lyrics by Irving Caesar and Otto Harbach, music by Vincent Youmans, book by Otto Harbach and Frank Mandel; 1971 revival, book adapted by Burt Shevelove.

Features tap dance and soft shoe set to the popular music of the 1920s. Tony Award, Best Choreography, 1971 (Donald Saddler, revival).

On Your Toes (1936/1954/1983)

Book by Richard Rodgers, George Abbott, and Lorenz Hart, music by Rodgers, and lyrics by Hart.

First dramatic use of classical dance (ballet) in a Broadway musical; 1936 and 1954 productions choreographed by George Balanchine.

Lady in The Dark (1941)

Music by Kurt Weill, lyrics by Ira Gershwin, book by Moss Hart.

Choreography by Albertina Rasch; all but the final song in the score performed in the context of three extensive dream sequences.

Oklahoma! (1943/1951/1979/2002)

Music by Richard Rodgers, book and lyrics by Oscar Hammerstein II.

Choreographed by Agnes de Mille; Act 1 ends in a 15-minute dream ballet.

On the Town (1944/1971/1998/2014)

> Music by Leonard Bernstein, book and lyrics by Betty Comden and Adolph Green. Choreography by Jerome Robbins, based on his ballet, *Fancy Free*. Ballet and extended dance sequences are integrated into the storytelling throughout the musical.

Carousel (1945/1949, 1994/2017)

> Music by Richard Rodgers, book and lyrics by Oscar Hammerstein II. Choreographed by Agnes de Mille, extended ballet sequence in Act 2.

> Tony Award, Best Choreography, 2018 (Justin Peck, revival)

West Side Story (1957/1960/1980/2009)

> Book by Arthur Laurents; music by Leonard Bernstein; lyrics byStephen Sondheim; conception, choreography, and direction by Jerome Robbins.

> Tony Award, Best Choreography, 1958.

> Comprised of more dancing than in any previous Broadway musical. Dancers given double the standard rehearsal period for the time (eight weeks instead of four) and given license to develop characters and act their roles rather than just embodying the choreography. Groundbreaking in terms of dance, music, and theatrical style.

Sweet Charity (1966/1986/2005)

> Music by Cy Coleman, lyrics by Dorothy Fields and book by Neil Simon.

> Conceived, directed and choreographed by Bob Fosse.

> Central character is a dancer-for-hire in a dance hall and much of the story is conveyed through dance. Showcases Fosse's distinctive style.

> Tony Award, Best Choreography, 1966.

Pippin (1972/2013)

> Music and lyrics by Stephen Schwartz , book by Roger O. Hirson..
>
> Directed and choreographed by Bob Fosse.
>
> The dance language of the show often carries its subtext and is credited with the show's longevity.
>
> Tony Award, Best Choreography, 1973.

A Chorus Line (1975/2006)

> Music by Marvin Hamlisch, lyrics by Edward Kleban, book by James Kirkwood, Jr. and Nicholas Dante. Directed and co-choreographed (with Bob Avian) by Michael Bennett.
>
> Based on interviews with dancers in a workshop setting. The show is set on a bare stage in a Broadway theater and follows seventeen dancers as they audition for places in the chorus line of a musical.
>
> Tony Award, Best Choreography, 1976.

My One and Only (1983)

> Book by Peter Stone and Timothy S. Mayer , music and lyrics by George and Ira Gershwin.
>
> Book musical in which the plot serves to unite a program of Gershwin material from their 1927 *Funny Face* and other popular shows. During tryouts director Peter Sellars was fired and replaced with lead actor Tommy Tune (who co-directed and co-choreographed with Thommie Walsh). Choreographer Michael Bennett also assisted with direction and choreography.
>
> Tony Award, Best Choreography, 1983.

Chicago (1975/1996)

> Music by John Kander, lyrics by Fred Ebb, book by Ebb and Bob Fosse. Directed and choreographed by Bob Fosse.

Each song modeled on a particular vaudeville number or performer.

Tony Award, Best Choreography, 1997.

Crazy for You (1992)

Book by Ken Ludwig, lyrics by Ira Gershwin, and music by George Gershwin. Directed by Mike Ockrent and choreographed by Susan Stroman.

Adaptation of Gershwins' 1930 *Girl Crazy*. Song and dance musical set in the era of the Follies.

Tony Award, Best Choreography, 1992.

The Lion King (1997)

Music by Elton John, lyrics by Tim Rice, book by Roger Allers and Irene Mecchi. Choreography by Garth Fagan.

A showcase of African, Caribbean, ballet and modern dance styles. Dancers perform wearing elaborate puppets much of the time.

Tony Award, Best Choreography, 1998.

Billy Elliott (2008)

Music by Elton John, book and lyrics by Lee Hall (screenwriter of the film).

Choreography by Peter Darling, who also created the choreography for the 2000 Stephen Daldry film.

Although the narrative hinges on a young boy discovering his gift and passion for ballet, tap and modern also feature prominently.

Tony Award, Best Choreography, 2009.

Fela! (2009/2012)

> Book by Bill T. Jones and Jim Lewis, based on music and lyrics by the late Nigerian singer Fela Kuti, with additional music by Aaron Johnson and Jordan McLean and additional lyrics by Jim Lewis.

> Choreography by Bill T. Jones grounded in AfroBeat, a blend of African, jazz, soul and funk music and dance styles.

> Tony Award, Best Choreography, 2010.

Little Dancer (2014)

> Music by Stephen Flaherty, book and lyrics Lynn Ahrens, Choreography by Susan Stroman.

> This show explores the imagined relationship between Edgar Degas and the young ballerina who posed for his famous sculpture, a role was originated by NYCB principal dancer Tiler Peck. This piece is still in development under the title *Marie, Dancing Still* and ran at the 5th Avenue Theater in Seattle in the spring of 2019.

An American in Paris (2015)

> Music by George Gershwin, lyrics by Ira Gershwin, book by Craig Lucas

> Choreography by Christopher Wheeldon.

> The film is famous for its 17-minute ballet sequence starring ballerina Leslie Caron and Gene Kelly. The musical uses the power of dance to carry and convey the story. Wheeldon and Jerome Robbins collaborated at NYCB, and his use of dance in this work is reminiscent of both Robbins' and Balanchine's choreography for the Broadway stage.

> Tony Award, Best Choreography, 2015.

Broadway Concert Musicals: Annotated

Dancin' (1978) Musical revue

> Directed and choreographed by Bob Fosse

> Bob Fosse's tribute to the art of dance. Set on primarily American music, employing a wide variety of dance genres and styles.

> Tony Award, Best Choreography, 1978.

Cats (1982/2016) Sung-through musical

> Music by Andrew Lloyd Webber, based on *Old Possum's Book of Practical Cats* by T.S. Eliot in addition to some of his other writings. Choreography by Gillian Lynne.

> Story and character conveyed through continuous movement and dance.

Stomp (1991) Off-Broadway theatrical show, music and movement, no dialogue

> Created by Steve McNicholas and Luke Cresswell

> Use of the body and ordinary objects to create dance, pantomime, and acrobatics.

Bring in 'da Noise, Bring in 'da Funk (1996) Musical revue

> Conceived and directed by George C. Wolfe; music by Daryl Waters, Zane Mark and Ann Duquesnay; lyrics by Reg E. Gaines, George C. Wolfe and Ann Duquesnay; book by Reg E. Gaines; choreography by Savion Glover.

> Musical revue telling the story of Black History from slavery to the present through tap dance.

> Tony Award, Best Choreography, 1996.

Fosse (1999) Musical revue, no dialogue or narration

> Conceived by Richard Maltby, Jr., Chet Walker, and Ann Reinking

> Three-act revue showcasing the original choreography of Bob Fosse performed by many of the dancers who had worked with him.

Swing! (1999) Musical, no dialogue

> Conceived by Paul Kelly with music by various artists.

> Celebration of the swing era of jazz told through dance, song, and acrobatics.

Movin' Out (2002) Jukebox musical, no dialogue

> Conceived by Twyla Tharp, music by Billy Joel.

> The story of a generation of young people in Long Island during the 1960s, told through music and dance.

> Tony Award, Best Choreography, 2003.

Burn the Floor (2009) Dance concert

> Conceived by Harley Metcalf, choreography by Jason Gilkison.

> A showcase of ballroom and social dancing.

Come Fly Away (2010) Musical revue, no dialogue

> Conceived, directed and choreographed by Twyla Tharp; the music of Frank Sinatra.

> Set in a New York City nightclub, the story follows four couples in their search for love and romance.

On Your Feet! (2015) Jukebox musical

> Book by Alexander Dinelaris, directed by Jerry Mitchell, the music of Gloria Estefan. Choreography by Sergio Trujillo.

The story of Emilio and Gloria Estefan, featuring the Cuban-fusion sound popularized by Gloria Estefan.

Outliers: Annotated

Contact (2000)

Developed by Susan Stroman and John Weidman, book by Weidman, choreography and direction by Stroman. Tony Award, Best Choreography, 2000.

Contact explores the nature of human contact in a three-act musical – what draws people together and what drives them apart. It was performed on Broadway by a cast of triple threat performers with resumes rich in both dance and theater experience. The show is comprised of three vignettes set in three distinct time periods spanning the 18th through the 20th centuries, leaving the audience with a sense of the universality of the nature of relationships across time.

The approach of the creative team turns the formula typical of Broadway musicals upside down. Where the book typically anchors the work and defines the story world, here it is the dance. Where music and dance typically provide the subtext, here the sparing use of dialogue provides the underpinning of a world where music and dance drive the narrative.

Synetic Theater (founded 2001)

Paata Tsikurishvili and Irina Tsikurishvili, Founding Artistic Director and Founding Choreographer.

With their shared backgrounds in dance, theater, and film as the basis, founding members Paata and Irina Tsikurishvili seek to tell classic stories in ways that rely on movement, music, and the visual arts. They endeavor to create visceral experiences for their audiences. Synetic's premiere performance was the first wordless Shakespeare production, a treatment of *Hamlet*, introducing a new brand of physical theater to the Washington DC metropolitan area. Part of their mission is to foster artistic growth, evident across their productions wherein actors are challenged in physical terms and dancers deliver performances nuanced in dramatic expression.

Stay (2011)

Book by Heather McDonald, choreography by Susan Shields.

Two-year collaboration in development at Theater of the First Amendment and Woolly Mammoth Theater before a limited run at the Lansburg Theater in Washington, DC. An exploration of an extended family as they stay, drift, reconcile, bond, mourn. A theater, dance, music, and multimedia production. Most striking was the cast, half actors and half dancers, who walked in one another's craft at various points in the play, advancing the narrative through both conventional acting and dance. Actors danced segments of the narrative and dancers used language rather than movement, each with skill and an utter lack of self-consciousness. In one remarkable sequence, a couple comes to terms with their several miscarriages as the woman dances in a costume layered with scarves, losing scarves as the dance progresses. This approach, of actors and dancers both working in their craft and stepping in and out of one another's, was in the forefront of my thinking as Meredith and I began our collaboration on *Fractals*.

Cagney (2016)

Music and lyrics by Robert Creighton and Christopher McGovern, book by Peter Colley, directed by Bill Castellino, choreography by Joshua Bergasse.

Robert Creighton's tour de force performance and labor of love, developed over a 20-year period and performed in a number of regional settings that preceded a healthy off-Broadway run of 502 performances. In addition to masterful tap performances by Creighton as James Cagney and Jeremy Benton as Bob Hope, the ensemble uses dance beyond its typical conventions in musical theater. For example, in parallel sequences, they use it to simulate the typewriters of the respective writers' rooms at Warner Brothers and Cagney Productions. Dance also works to establish setting and time passage in this epic treatment of Cagney's life, including vaudeville, movie musicals, and USO show-style production numbers. The gifted ensemble members play multiple roles with equal facility to their expert dancing.

Prior to the shutdown of live theater due to the Covid-19 pandemic, Cagney was barreling toward its West End (London) premiere and expects to resume that journey when live theater resumes.

Paramour, Cirque de Soleil (2016)

Written, directed and choreographed by Philippe Decouflé.

Paramour was Cirque de Soleil's first resident musical, enjoying a successful one-year run on Broadway. Set in 1930s Hollywood, it follows café singer Indigo through the emergence of her career as a movie star to the point where she most choose between the director who established her and the man she loves. The show featured 10 original songs and the acrobatic spectacle familiar to Cirque de Soleil audiences. At times these performances served in the capacity of an ensemble, establishing the story world of the musical. At times they commented on the action, deepening its meaning or creating visual metaphor.

Dance Theater

The origins of dance theater most likely occur with the Bauhaus Art Movement in the 1920s and 1930s; specifically, a 1932 Paris competition which pitted Oskar Schlemmer's *Triadisches Ballet* against Kurt Jooss' *The Green Table*, among others. Schlemmer shaped the Bauhaus theater movement with his dance pieces; Jooss was one of the founders of Tanztheater (dance theater) which combined movement, text and drama.

The *Triadisches Ballet* is divided mathematically among three dancers who each dance a solo, a duet, and a trio. The piece is set to avant-garde music composed by Paul Hindemith, with futuristic costuming that bears a strong resemblance to those favored by the contemporary Cirque de Soleil. Much of it is mechanical, Schlemmer favoring the movements of puppets and the use of blank facial expressions over the fluidity of expression typical of dance at the time.

The Green Table stands out as perhaps the earliest example of dancers acting and actors dancing. Jooss abandons many of the conventions of dance and costumes his dancers as real people: as refugees, as prostitutes. The women wear their hair down and dance on flat or barefoot rather than en pointe. *The Green Table* speaks to a political dilemma, the futility of peace negotiations during a time of war, and it is anti-war in its position. The subject matter in itself was revolutionary for its time. During his career, Jooss frequently engaged civil rights conflicts: by refusing to expel Jewish dancers from his studio under the Nazi Regime, and by refusing to perform in segregated theaters upon arriving in the United States. His protégés include Mary Wigman and Pina Bausch, both instrumental to the evolution of modern dance worldwide.

The term dance theater is usually attributed to the work of Pina Bausch, based on her revolutionary approach to making dances that have their origins in the experiences and the gestures of her dancers. Previously referenced in this chapter, Synetic Theater refers to their work as "theater that moves." Even though the dance theater genre is unwieldy both conceptually and in terms of defining or characterizing it, at its core it is always theater that moves.

Synetic produced its 14th in a series of Wordless Shakespeare plays (Richard III) during their 2018-2019 season. Theater Bay Area reported a California Shakespeare Theater production of *Midsummer*

Night's Dream that used modern dance and movement to "deepen their connection to the play's truths."

One of the primary aspects of dance theater that sets it apart from musical theater (theater dance) is its endeavor to set the music on the dancer; to derive the movement from the dancers' bodies, experiences, and ways of moving. Meredith Barnes works in this capacity with the dancers of DanceArtTheater, and both she and Amanda Whiteman did so in the creation of *Fractals*. This practice utilizes the physical vocabulary of the performers in the room, invites them to grow as artists, fosters collaboration, and ultimately expands the performance vocabulary of the audience. Many artists also use this genre as a forum for collapsing multiple art forms including dance, movement, text, music, and multimedia (cf. previously referenced production, *Stay*). The genre also experiments with the physical relationship between the performers and the audience and is frequently site-specific.

The incorporation of text is an essential element of dance theater and is present in the work of many contemporary choreographers. Bausch frequently used it in her work. We used it in *Fractals*. Sean Dorsey, a San Francisco-based choreographer, layered his 2014 *Secret History of Love* with both recorded interviews clips and spoken text from his interview transcripts. He feels the use of text makes the dance more accessible, that it "provides the audience with a window into the work."

New York-based choreographer Jack Ferver incorporates text into all of his work, which he frequently writes and performs himself. In hiring dancers, he stresses the need for honesty and fearlessness in addition to dance and vocal technique. In keeping with the genre, the relationship between his performers and audiences remains fluid.

Autumn Eckman, currently on the dance faculty of the University of Arizona, set part of her 2015 piece *Sardine* on Steven Stogatz's TEDTalk about synchronization in nature (a phenomenon that is coincidentally fractal). Bill T. Jones premiered a piece early in 2020 that layered passages from Melville's *Moby Dick* with Martin Luther King's *I Have A Dream* speech (delivered backwards, at times) to explore the tension that exists between community and isolation, particularly during divisive political times. This piece was originally titled *What Problem?* Jones continues to develop it under the title *Deep Blue Sea*.

In *Fractals*, the use of spoken word conjures imagery that informs the choreography and establishes rhythm to coax and propel the movement. The possibilities are endless.

COLLABORATION: ACTING AND DANCE

In the 40 years that I have been an actor, director, and acting teacher, it never occurred to me that actors and dancers understand acting differently, that they communicate and conceptualize it differently, and that their acting training differs greatly. I didn't even realize it during the time we spent working on *Fractals*.

The question emerged from the research for this book, prompted by a passage in Larry Stempel's *Showtime*. Jerome Robbins trained at The Actor's Studio and came to wonder, "what the difference was in the source of expression for acting as opposed to dancing." He began to use the Method acting techniques he learned there in his work, both in ballet and on Broadway. I began to ask dancers about this, and I realized how far removed the experience of actors and dancers is. It is critical to understand this in order for actors and dancers (and directors and choreographers) to collaborate to their greatest potential.

Dance and Movement for Actors

Even within the acting community, there is broad diversity in training and approach. Suffice to say that movement is a very small part of most actors' training, and their training may not include dance at all if they are not studying musical theater.

Neither in my high school nor college experience was dance training included in the curriculum. The expectation was for student actors to seek dance training on their own. This is unfortunate. Actors tend to be more in their heads than in their bodies, and the beginning of their training would be an excellent time to explore the potential of physical expression more rigorously.

I was on staff at an audition once with choreographer and dance instructor Elizabeth "Buffy" Price. While the actors who auditioned lacked training and technique, she was impressed by the extent to which they were willing to throw themselves into the work. She remarked that dancers tend to be careful when working on new choreography, that they focus on doing it correctly and broaden their expression later. Actors jump right in.

This has not always been my experience, with actors or with dancers, but it raises the point that there needs to be a willingness to risk when learning something new, whether that be new material in one's own discipline, or the demands of another discipline altogether.

There are also myriad techniques and philosophies in the acting community regarding the practice of acting. I advocate exploring them all and dropping the ones that work into a toolbox rather than espousing any one approach. I will offer, as a bottom line, that the practice is about action rather than emotion. It is called acting, not emoting.

What many outside the profession do not understand is that by committing to an action within a scene, something one is determined to accomplish within the given circumstances of the play and the truth of the moment, that the actor's emotional life will emerge naturally from the work. There is no need to plan it, manufacture it, or force it.

When acting is allowed to manifest in this way, based on the human interaction between actors onstage, it is honest and organic, a living thing, an extension of our humanity. Less experienced actors tend to make decisions about how they feel at a given moment in the text or decide in advance how they will deliver certain lines – or worse yet, be directed in this manner.

There is also a lot of misconception about what constitutes Method acting and to what extent this is an advisable approach. This is not the place to examine this enormous question, but the work of Konstantin Stanislavski (1863-1938) is the place to start for anyone eager to understand Method acting in its purest and most practical sense. Sonia Moore's excellent resource, *The Stanislavski System*, is an accessible point of entry. Stanislavski advocated that actors play the action of a given scene and let the emotional life of the scene emerge authentically.

Acting for Dancers

Actor/dancer Paula Leggett Chase once told me, "It is harder to find actors who dance than it is to find dancers who act." This is most evident in terms of musical theater, or any other creative environment where dancers and actors work collaboratively.

In many of my experiences observing dancers in rehearsal, directors and choreographers ask for emotional expression of some sort. Sometimes they seek to elicit the illustration of emotion as an integral component of the dancers' technique; sometimes they are simply layering it over the movement. I imagine that the latter occurs because dancers are given as little training in acting as actors are in movement and dance, unless they seek it explicitly. I became curious about this and discussed it with several dance professionals. This is what I learned.

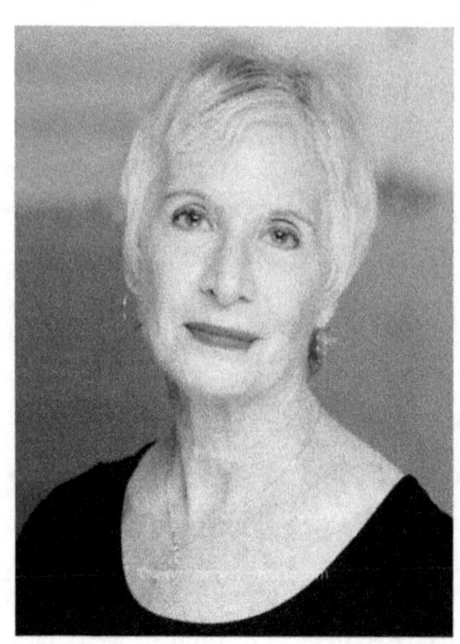

Constance Walsh

Photo credit: John Nelson

Constance Walsh is a dancer, choreographer, and dance instructor currently on the faculty of BalletNova in Northern Virginia. She also serves as its Director of Enrichment and Adult

Programs, and Principal of its Pre-Professional Division. As a young dancer she studied with Daniel Nagrin before moving to New York to attend the Martha Graham School of Contemporary Dance on scholarship. Martha Graham selected her work for the Young Choreographers Series in 1975. She created two dance companies and ran her own studio before coming to BalletNova.

Her classes are challenging, joyful and dynamic. I have had the pleasure of dancing with her and of speaking with her on more than one occasion about dance and dance education.

Walsh confirmed repeatedly that there is not enough training in acting for dancers, and that in lieu of it, dancers tend to glean it from their directors, choreographers, or someone who has danced a given role before them. She expressed concern that a lot of the art is getting lost as dancers lean more heavily on video to learn choreography and roles, one of the liabilities being that their performances become an imitation of someone else's work rather than an expression of their own artistry.

Her earliest training was in ballet. She was introduced to modern dance in a summer program at Johnson State College (Vermont) under the instruction of modern dancer and choreographer Daniel Nagrin (1917-2008).

That summer she took classes in acting and improvisation. She recalled that they were terrifying, but they changed her life. She reflected that in ballet, you are typically part of a group, that your individuality is not the focus of the work, but that her summer with Nagrin was an environment designed for students to take risks and discover themselves, to "find out who [we] were."

In her work with Martha Graham, she recalled that Graham was "all about acting," that she was clear in communicating her vision, and that this vision was rooted in the movement, the story, and the character. She referred me to Graham's published notebooks (1973), rich not only as a choreographic record but in the stories, literary quotations, and studies that gave her work dimension and life.

Walsh summarized by saying that when she goes to a performance she wants to be moved, and that comes from something being told – perhaps story, perhaps the emotional life of the character – but something in which every movement means something.

She also mentioned her son Connor Walsh, a principal dancer with the Houston Ballet. She said that he is frequently coached in the acting of a particular role, but that he never feels that he gets enough of this emphasis. In one of his first roles, Lynsky in *Eugene Onegrin*, he was coached in acting through movement – for example, being asked to articulate what Lynsky was saying when he does a pirouette. This kind of approach could serve both dancers and actors well, to marry an understanding of the physical life to the interior life of a character.

Walsh shared that in her own work as a choreographer, she uses imagery with dancers and students that may not relate to the character but to the individual. She is the most engaged by stories and storytelling, and she endeavors to invest her dancers in this, in trying to say something about the human condition through movement. She echoes the notion that dancers tend to be preoccupied with technique, with correctness, but also underlined the need to invest the physical manifestation of the character with a rich, real interior life.

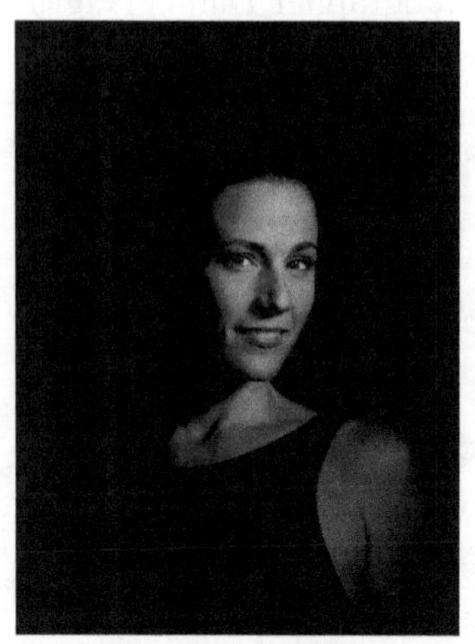

Autumn Eckman
Photo credit: Andrew Yew

Autumn Eckman is a dancer, choreographer, and dance instructor. She is currently an Assistant Professor of Dance at the University of Arizona. She received her classical training at the Houston Ballet Academy and has danced professionally with a number of companies (State Street Ballet, Cangelosi Dance Project, Lucky Plush Productions, Luna Negra Dance Theater, Hubbard Street Dance Chicago, Ron De Jesus

Dance, Collective Body Dance Lab). She was a resident choreographer for Giordano Dance Chicago and has been commissioned by several dance companies, dance schools, and universities.

Eckman reinforced the notion that dancers do not receive formal training in acting or voice. She said that some dancers study the basic tenets of acting, and some are exposed to improv – which is important to generating spontaneous movement as a dancer, the ability to answer a choreographer's prompt or another dancer's movement with, "Yes, and…"

This and other techniques practiced in an improv setting can be borrowed and translated into movement, into a dancer's physicality. She also noted that although it tends not to be part of their training, dancers are being asked to use their voices more and more. Eckman herself incorporates a great deal of spoken text into her work, and due to the theatricality of post-modern dance and dance theater, dancers must know how to act in some capacity. She feels they must learn it even through coaching while working on a piece, that they must be able to express themselves through gesture, tone, and mood.

She also pointed out that classical dancers carry the narrative of a given production through pantomime, that their training is in the complete reliance of physicality to convey a story. This background tends to produce dancers who want to know exactly what they are going to be doing and what is being asked of them, while some are looser and more responsive to a request for spontaneity, risk-taking, and collaboration. She suggested that the rehearsal environment has a great deal to do with the dancers' ability to work as actors, and to adapt to new and changing demands on their creativity.

Eckman spent two winters working with a program that trains actors in Meyerhold technique. Meyerhold was a contemporary of Stanislavski and pioneered a technique he originally referred to as biomechanics but later called physical theater. He taught that the emotional life of an actor was linked to his physical state and worked from the outside in to access and express those emotions.

Eckman initially presented the biomechanics of dance at this conference but was so fascinated by the work that she returned the following year to teach contact improv. She found these actors to be willing to rid themselves of hesitation and inhibition, and rely on their own organic movement, even as they worked from bodies that were essentially untrained. Because the students came from all over the world, primarily Europe and South America, they often had no common language except for movement. She described a process by which actors built a story through time, space, negative space, and levels, essentially writing a script without using words.

There was a gap of several years between my interviews with her. She mentioned in the second one that in that time, dancers were becoming more aware of intention in their work, that they were becoming more mindful of their objectives in a given dance, similar to the ways in which actors approach scene work. She sees this as an important advancement, a way to work from intention rather than indication, a way to show rather than tell.

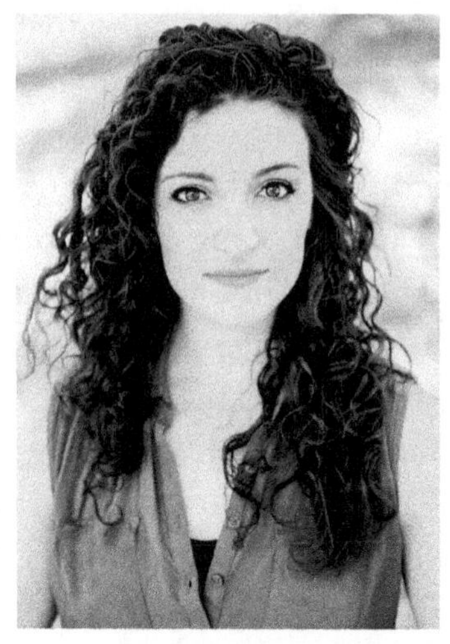

Jessi Shull
Photo credit: Megan Schmitz

Jessi Shull is a dancer, arts educator, and choreographer living and working in the Washington DC metro area. She is a member of the DanceArtTheater company and is a dancer and manager with Dancin' Unlimited Jazz Dance Company. She is a 2013 graduate of Elon University. When she began college, she discovered that the head of the acting department had never taught dancers before, which resulted in their exposure to Meisner technique. She feels this one class changed the way she behaves onstage, that it has enabled her to behave realistically in an imaginary world.

Shull echoed some of Autumn Eckman's remarks, noting the different approaches in classical ballet and modern dance with regard to acting. Classical dance relies on pantomime and storytelling and must be larger than life due to the enormity of the performance spaces ballet companies inhabit. Modern dance tends to be vague in terms of purpose and character, so the dancer must supply those if the director/choreographer does not. She asserts that a dancer must connect with the character being played, that technique alone is not enough to engage and hold an audience.

Because she works as an actor and singer in addition to her dancing, she sees the differences first-hand in the way actors and dancers work. She finds that actors are more mental than physical, that with dancers, "their body gets there before their mind does." This gives the appearance that dancers are picking up the work more quickly, but they may just be using a different aptitude, a different way of knowing.

Shull values the challenge of being fully present whenever one is onstage, regardless of whether or not that person is focal in a given moment. She appreciates actors who remain engaged and dancers who resist being "dead in the face and body" when they do not have specific choreography in the course of a performance. She feels that the power of storytelling is what drives the work for her, no matter the discipline, genre or style. She is honored to be the conduit for other people's stories as well as her own.

Tomé Cousin is currently an associate professor of dance at Carnegie Mellon University, one aspect of a long

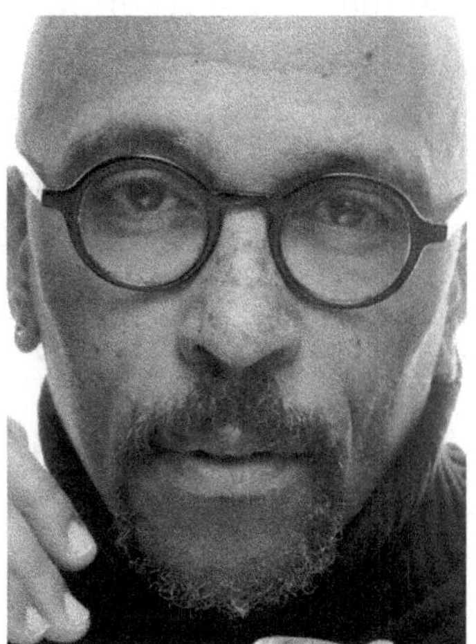

Tomé Cousin
Photo credit: Curtis Reaves

and storied career. Among his creative mentors he includes Susan Stroman, Martha Clarke, George C. Wolfe, Ruth Maleczeh, Wendell Harrington, Luigi, Fred Rogers, John Weidman, Bertrum Ross, Miquel Goudreau, Hector Mercado, Judith Leifer, Bill T. Jones and Arnie Zane, Hope Clarke, Pina Bausch, Theo Bleckmann, Blondell Cummings, and Meredith Monk. He has composed more than 70 original theater, dance, musical, opera, film, and installation works for performance. He works as a performer, choreographer, director, writer, and educator.

Cousin appeared for nine seasons as Ragdoll Tomé on *Mister Rogers' Neighborhood* and went on to direct two of Fred Rogers' original, one-act operas for Pittsburgh Festival Opera in the summer of 2019. An original cast member of the Tony Award winning musical *Contact*, Cousin traveled the world from 2006-2017 setting Susan Stroman's choreography on new productions of the work.

Cousin has been on faculty at Carnegie Mellon for ten years and finds it supportive of his desire to be a Total Theater Artist and to teach others to strive for this ideal. He defines this as "one who is equally comfortable with dance, drama, technology, speech, direction, and music, filtered through the ever-changing landscape of computer and film technology."

Being a Total Theater Artist is a tall order to fill. All students, whether concentrating on drama or musical theater, receive extensive movement training in Laban Movement, Horton Technique, Suzuki Movement, Clown Workshop, and ballet. While there is no dance major or minor available at Carnegie Mellon, Cousin says that the students' dance training is intense and that his goal is to over-train them so that there will be no choreography or movement in their future that they cannot handle.

Cousin maintains that actors and dancers experience different challenges. Actors come to movement with a certain amount of intimidation in place, while dancers often have some unlearning to do. Either way, he feels his first job is to earn their trust. He finds that actors tend to jump into the work while dancers tend to listen for complete instruction before proceeding. He credits this to the environment in which dancers are trained: They are expected to listen and follow directions, and there is little talk in the studio. Actors are accustomed to taking risks; dancers often have to learn to feel comfortable speaking their names aloud at an audition or offering input during a rehearsal.

Cousin also describes what he calls the "arrested development" of dancers who, even as adults, are often referred to as "boys and girls." He prefers "folks, people, gang, y'all," rather than suggesting that his dancers are children who need to do as they're told rather than engage in the process.

He addresses the acting work intrinsic to dance the same way with actors and dancers. He teaches them to analyze a movement text (non-verbal text) in terms of motivation, objective, and gesture. Cousin draws a clear distinction between pantomime and organic movement. Pantomime is a starting point, the drawing of big, bold gestures to convey an idea. Organic movement goes deeper. It is movement derived from purpose-driven action, from pursuing an objective, from having something visceral and complicated to communicate.

I asked him for clarification of this distinction, and he responded with an exercise he learned while working with Pina Bausch at the Tanztheater Wuppertal. Performers work on monologues until they know them well, then they begin to alternate movement for every other line of text. They understand that they are not to pantomime the content of the missing sentences; they are to express them through organic movement. After they can alternate sentences, they begin to experiment with using words and movement intermittently, letting the material inhabit their bodies so that movement and speech become interwoven means of pursuing an objective. Cousin uses this exercise in the classroom as well as in professional settings.

Cousin refers to himself as a Total Theater Artist and as an interdisciplinary artist and considers the divisions in the performing arts to be artificial. He envisions this type of performer as a triangle, with each angle represented by movement, acting, and singing. Depending on the individual, the top of the triangle will differ – the person will be a natural dancer or singer or actor. This is a reflection of training and innate talent. The top of the triangle may need to shift given the demands of the production at hand; a natural singer may need to train until dance is equally strong, a natural dancer may have to strengthen acting skills until movement is accomplishing more than conveying story.

Cousin posited that the reality television phenomenon has resulted in more triple threat performers being in the marketplace, because they see others push boundaries and assume they can do it as well. Because he sees the division between the performing arts as artificial, he believes they can bleed into one another; they can blend. They can also be shut off, one's full attention being given to say, dancing the dying swan, going "full technique." Being a triple threat is as much about knowing where to focus for a given performance as it is having the capacity to do multiple things well.

Cousin was one of the 19 original cast members of Stroman and Weidman's *Contact*, first in workshops and later on Broadway, the Tony Award winner for Best Musical in 2000 (See Chapters 2 and 5 for more regarding *Contact*). All 19 were triple threat performers, which Cousin acknowledges is difficult. You really have to want it, and you have to want to be continually training and growing and learning. You do not arrive.

Even if you are a dancer first, there is always more to learn, more styles, more agility, more range. If you are a singer, you can master multiple genres, improve your technique, adapt your sound. I asked him about following the run of *Contact* with a long career of setting Stroman's choreography on dance companies around the world. For the first of these productions, at Virginia Stage Company in Norfolk, Virginia, he cast performers who had already done the show – in workshops, on Broadway, in the National Tour, in a student production he directed at Point Park University in Pittsburgh. He leaned heavily on one of the swings from the Broadway company, who knew all the women's roles.

After completing this, he had a process, a way to go about it. Many of the subsequent productions were co-produced by theater and ballet companies. Cousin's primary tasks as he toured the world became: bringing actors up to speed on the enormous demands of the dancing; teaching primarily ballet dancers the many different styles of movement in the show and getting them comfortable with speaking onstage; and making the stories resonate with international audiences.

I was intrigued by this notion. What adaptations did he need to make for the stories to resonate? As with *Fractals*, the performers in *Contact* had to be clear in their understanding before the stories could convey. Part One is based on Fragonard's painting "The Swing," so the cast needed to be familiar with the painting and its cultural position. Part Two requires a familiarity with American pop culture in the 1950s, specifically Lucille Ball style comedy and the husband-wife dynamics intrinsic to it. Part Three was the most accessible because most of the cast was familiar with living in a big city.

Cousin found they needed to understand what New York City is really like rather than the way the city is depicted in films. Dramaturgy is critically important. It is so easy to take for granted that we are all viewing story through a common lens.

Creating a safe environment where the performers could trust Cousin and one another was key. He begins his rehearsals with a ritual where everyone (cast, staff, technicians) forms a circle and claps – one unified clap – and rehearsals end the same way.

As he explains it, everything between the claps is risk-free. He tells his performers that they will use every mistake they make. If something is wrong, it will be fixed. There is no right or wrong in the moment. Keep going. If you forget something, make something up. Everything done in a rehearsal is based on "yes," in pursuit of "yes," not about the individual performers but about the material.

To get actors moving, he reminds them that the body communicates non-verbally. We speak in movement text in the course of our daily lives. Dancers tend to focus on story and emotion in the course of a ballet, so to move them more solidly into acting, he focuses on dramaturgy. He adds layers of historical background, the meanings of words, whatever will help them understand the story world more completely, deeper than just the narrative itself. He considers it a cliché (a common one in musical theater) that we sing, or we dance when speaking is no longer enough.

Cousin maintains that what we should be doing in those moments is making the audience move; not moving them but making them move. He explained that the audience can be sitting back in their seats, observers of a presentation, or the performers can pull them into the experience, engaging them energetically. The drama and emotion intrinsic to the play already have them engaged, what Cousin calls being "forward in the work." The moments when people sing and dance in a musical are when the cast pulls the audience in, bringing them deeper into the work, connecting the energy between what is happening on the stage and what is happening in front of it. Live performance is unique in its capacity to form this connection.

Collaboration

Under ideal circumstances, *Fractals* would have been the type of collaboration in which actors and dancers worked side by side, each working in the craft of the other. Due to our time constraints and other variables, we only scratched the surface of this intention. What actually resulted was more the type of collaboration where each of us brings our own strength to the work and contributes from our expertise.

The company of DanceArtTheater acts as part of their regular practice; director Meredith Barnes coaches them and gives them homework to build into the work. Many of the company members also have acting experience. Our cast members had varying amounts

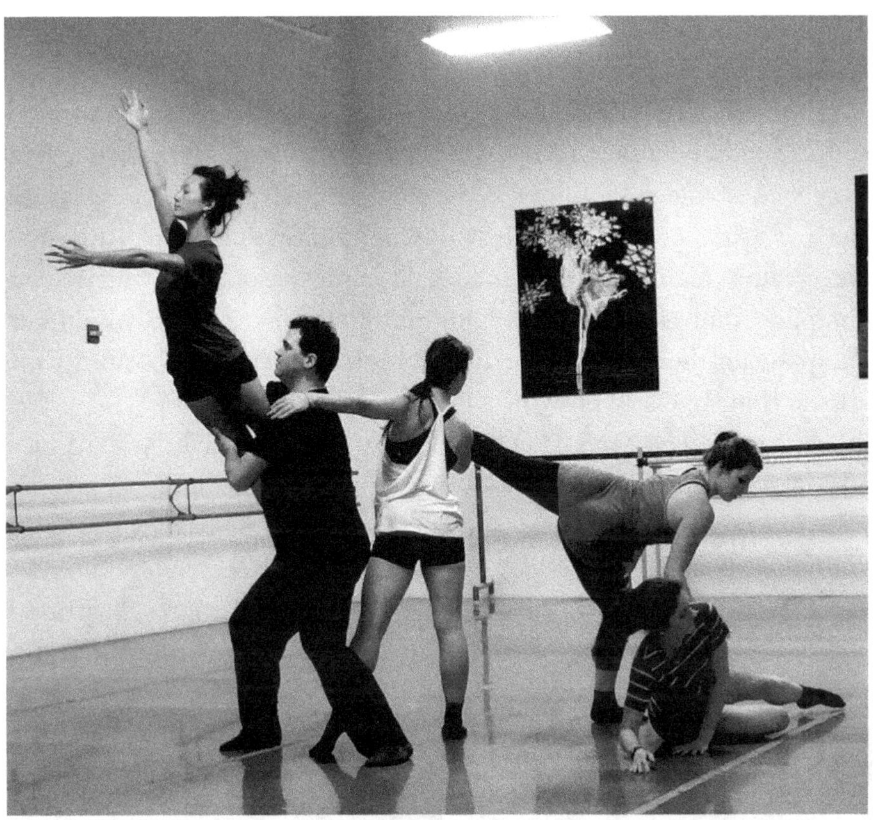

Fractals in rehearsal
Photo credit: Meredith Barnes

of dance training, and engaged more in movement than in actual dance, although Barnes worked the cast into some of the dances (and included the cast in her company classes during the rehearsal period).

The summer following *Fractals*, Meredith Barnes participated in a cross-disciplinary collaborative experience that became her next Fringe Festival production. Studio Theater and CulturalDC (Washington, DC) host an annual event called the Artistic Blind Date, partnering three artists from different disciplines to create a piece of performance art that is presented to the public in a festival setting. They met for the first time in December 2016 and by June 2017 performed for an audience, crafting a production on a given theme.

Working with the theme "covert catalyst," Barnes collaborated with composer-musician Mark Platenberg and actor-director Chelsea Thaler to create a half-hour show that they developed into a larger piece, *Through the Wall*, for the 2018 Capital Fringe Festival. Although the creative team makes their artistic contributions from their own disciplines (at least in this case) they are often performing beyond their discipline for the actual production. This is an exciting opportunity for artistic challenge and growth.

Artist Marcel Artes Deolazo, who works primarily in ceramics and illustration, shared with me his experience using an approach called *quattro mani*, or "four hands." He occasionally partners with another artisan in his work and they create pieces collaboratively. He showed me ceramic cups he had made (in this case illustrated

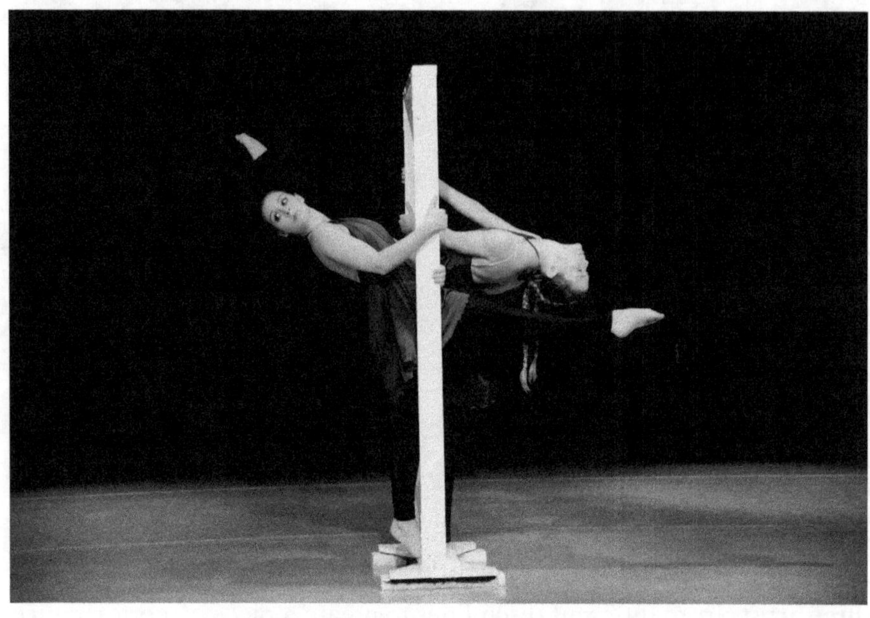

Through The Wall
Photo credit: Ruth Judson

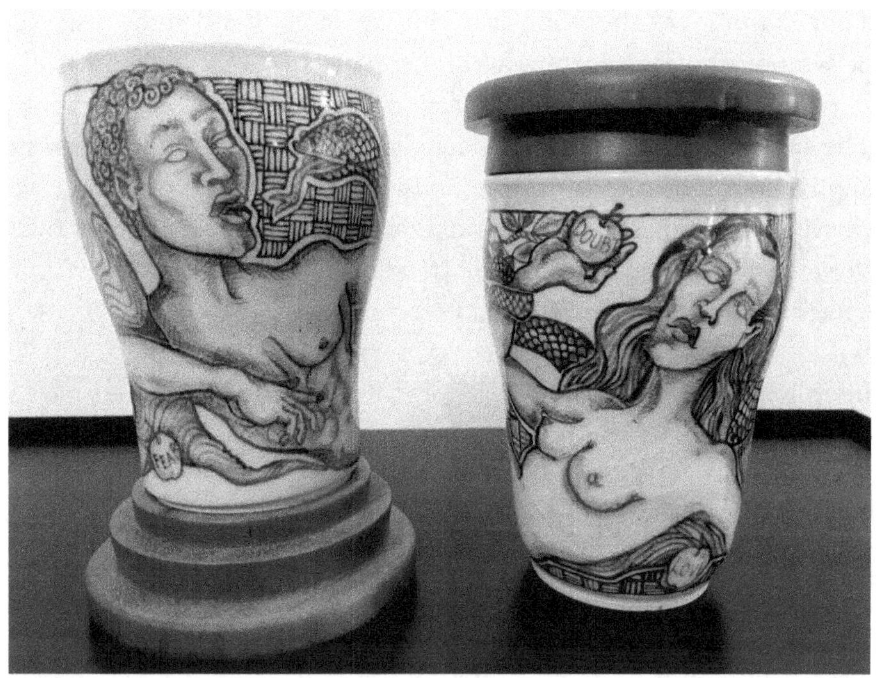

Adam and Eve, by Marcel Deolazo and wood turner Kevin Sherlock
Photo credit: Kimberley Cetron

with Adam and Eve) in partnership with a wood turner, who created bases for the cups that double as lids and are an artistic complement to Deolazo's work.

Silvia Bigliazzi and Sharon Wood edited a collection of essays under the title *Collaboration in the Arts from the Middle Ages to the Present*, which I reference in detail in the Introduction to this book. Collaboration is a complex cultural and political phenomenon: the combined practice of two or more artists, simultaneously or across time, or the willing collusion implied by the term's specifically historical meaning. These interdisciplinary essays propose collaboration as a strategy for ensuring creativity within a dynamic tradition, and as a means of mutual enrichment both between individuals and between disciplines.

They examine collaboration as tradition, ideology and in the contexts of symbolism, class, agency, and imagination.

There are chapters on *quattro mani* and on theatrical collaboration. The single greatest point they make is that collaboration is varied in approach and allows us to accomplish more in partnership than we can alone, whether we work in one another's crafts, bring our own strengths to bear on a given project, or dovetail the beginning of our efforts and the work of those who preceded us.

Interdisciplinary artist and educator Tomé Cousin introduced me to several collaborative projects involving innovator Bill T. Jones. In 1983 graphic artist Keith Haring body-painted Jones and photographer Tseng Kwong Chi captured his movements to music. Chi prompted Jones during the session in such a way that the photographs make statements about truth, fiction, and identity. These images have become iconic across all three of these artists' disciplines and beyond.

In 1999, Bill T. Jones collaborated with digital media artists Paul Kaiser and Shelly Eshkar on a project called *Ghostcatching*. Kaiser and Eshkar were already experimenting with motion-capture technology on the dances of choreographer Merce Cunningham. In some ways, joining their approach to Jones's is an extension of his earlier work with Haring and Chi. Kaiser and Eshkar created the visual and sound composition; Jones, the dance and vocal phrases. At times, Jones's body is multiplied into many dancers. The piece examines the experiences of being captured and breaking free. Multiple examples of this project are available by searching YouTube for *Ghostcatching*.

Through his work with Pina Bausch, Cousin was also familiar with a creative exercise that has the potential to be used across theater, dance, writing, and education environments. Imagine that a larger work is being developed, perhaps on the theme "Loss of Love." Each company member writes a personal account of an experience with this kind of loss and reads the work aloud. The group asks questions and offers similar experiences, points of connection, contrasts. The piece is then given to a different member of the company for choreography. In this way, the entire group has contributed, and one person is telling another person's lived experience through movement. This is a fascinating, complex, sophisticated approach to creativity, storytelling, and collaboration.

Workhouse Arts Center (Lorton, VA) sponsored an exciting collaborative arts initiative in November 2020 in which Tom Teasley (world percussion), Chao Tian (Chinese dulcimer), and Shu-Chen Cuff (contemporary dance) responded to the visual art installations on exhibit at Workhouse Arts under the organizing principle of "Reshaping Space." They conducted a virtual workshop a week before the performance and incorporated the audience response from that event into the production, allowing the audience to join them as collaborators in the work. This

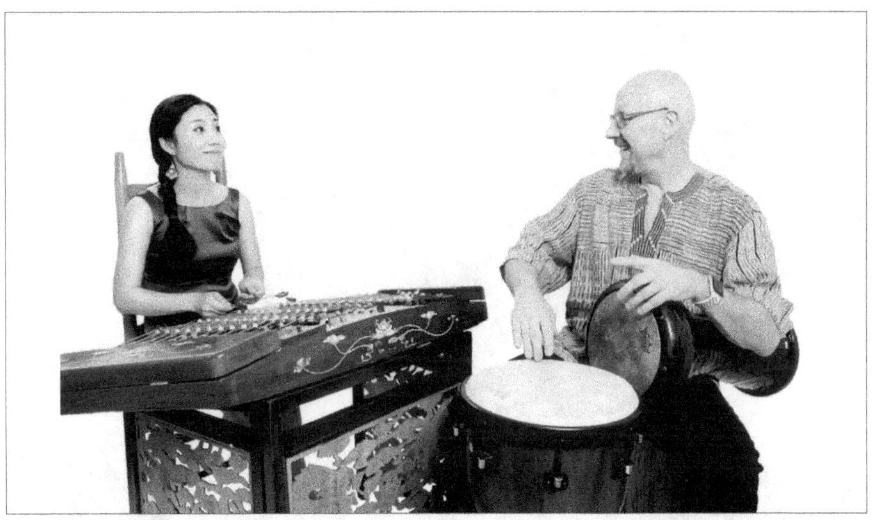

Chao Tian and Tom Teasley
Photo credit: Chia Chi (Charlie) Chang

program was entirely improvisational but had the polished look of work that had undergone extensive rehearsal.

I came to learn that Teasley and Tian view their work together as "musical dialogue," in which one asks a question musically and the other answers. While no one leads the dialogue, Tian says that she deliberately avoids leading because the melodic instrument in a duet tends to dominate. Teasley expresses what each of them does as developing a vocabulary and having a conversation, in time learning one another's language.

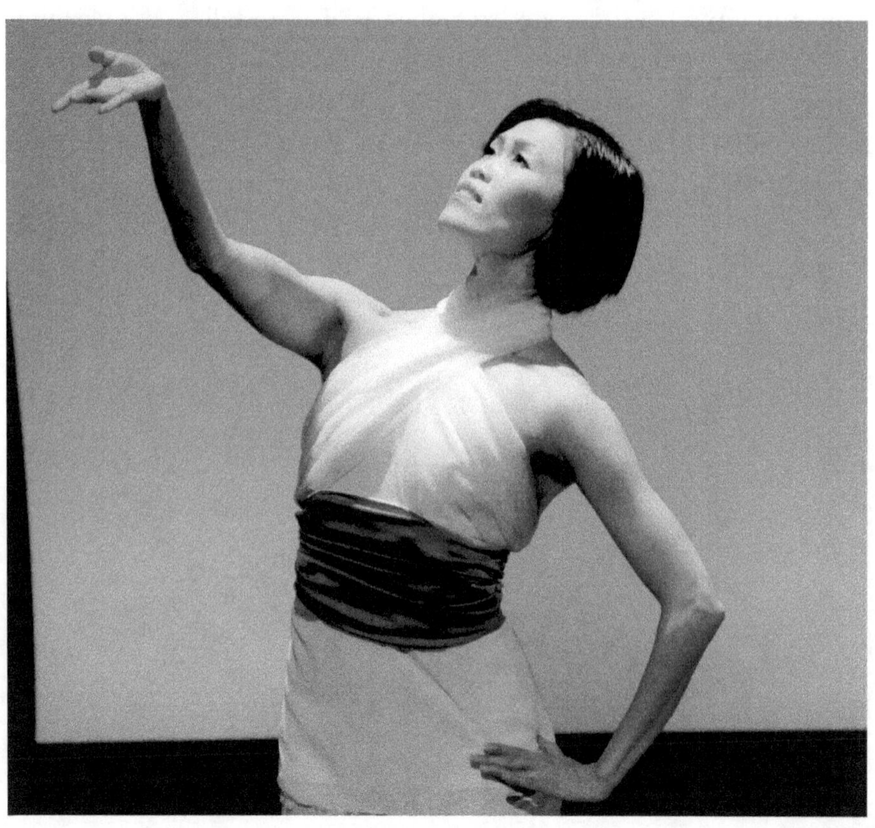

Shu-Chen Cuff
Photo credit: Ruth Judson

Both musicians emphasize the importance of listening, in real life and in music, to what the other is saying – as an expression of respect, and to inform the way one responds to the other. Tian articulated the Chinese aesthetic concept of Liu Bai, translated as leaving space or leaving blankness; she further explained that as one listens more and plays less, enlightenment and conflict resolution occur as natural results. This concept underpins a profound truth about the value of collaboration not just for artistic exploration and expression, but also in the application of the arts to other endeavors where communication and understanding are sought.

Dancer Shu-Chen Cuff is a classically trained dancer who incorporates elements of ballet, modern dance, Chinese Opera movement, Taiwanese Native dance, and African dance into her contemporary dance expression. In this production, Teasley, Tian, and Cuff all respond in real time to the ideas invoked by a given piece of artwork.

The alignment in their work is captivating. Cuff translates musical ideas as she experiences them into physical expressions of emotion, thought, and conversational interplay. At times the artwork on display also plays a role in the improvisational nature of the work. For example, in her porcelain coilwork piece "White Clouds," artist Laurel Lukaszewski installs more than 200 pieces of coil as a freestanding work using friction and very few nails. Once it is taken down, it will never exist in the same way again. In addition to the way this dynamic functions in live theater, Teasley, Tian and Cuff extend the temporal and visceral nature of collaborative performance by working through improvisation. A given performance will only exist in a given moment in time.

WRITING

Knowing where to begin with *Fractals* proved difficult. The challenge was to go beyond the idea of playwriting and consider ways to use

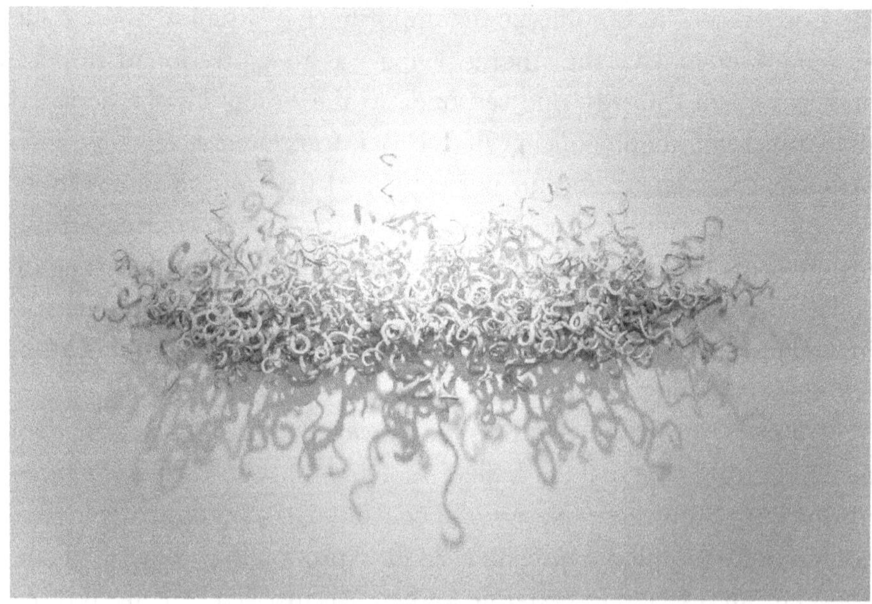

Laurel Lukaszewski, "White Clouds"
Photo credit: Audrey Miller

language in conjunction with Meredith's concept and choreography to create theater. We spoke about the work, and studied fractals together, until I started to hear the language in my mind. I was unaware of the practice of *quattro mani* at the time, but in retrospect, I see that is exactly what we were doing.

More than our four hands became involved in the work, primarily those of choreographer Amanda Whiteman, and certainly the cast and company members as well. One of my core beliefs as a writer is that content should drive form rather than the other way around, contrary to the writing approaches typically taught in academic settings.

I am in favor of getting the content on the page in whatever form it takes and determining the form it needs to assume to serve its purpose and audience. In this case, we worked through both poetry and a prose adaptation (to clarify meaning for the cast, late in the rehearsal process) and progressed from written to spoken language, from spoken language to closed captioning and American Sign Language (ASL).

The closed captioning required because we were housed at Gallaudet University (a private university serving the Deaf and hard of hearing community) added an interesting layer of meaning in that the written language and spoken language occurred simultaneously, so that the hearing audience was consuming both. This, and the challenge of grasping poetic language on a first hearing, is likely what led many audience members to request that we share the script with them in written form.

In terms of writing education, this script can serve as a model for several sound pedagogical practices: the exploration of academic concepts through multiple genres, playwriting on actors rather than for actors, revision as a dynamic and integral part of the writing process, and multigenre writing.

Exploring academic subjects through multiple genres

I attended a workshop once at which a high school science teacher shared an exercise that I have adapted and used over time. He asked his students to fold a sheet of paper into quarters. In the first quarter, he asked for a non-fiction paragraph about a scientific term or concept (ex, photosynthesis). Then he asked them to draw an illustration in the next square. Then he asked for a poem about the term or concept in the third square. Then he asked for a paragraph of fiction writing in which the term or concept was used.

This approach accomplishes so many objectives. It ensures that students thoroughly understand the concept. It uses different regions of the brain and different intelligences in its expression. It calls upon creativity in problem solving. It shows the student the concept viewed through different lenses, presented almost as puzzle pieces, parts of a whole.

All of the writing in *Fractals* forced me to understand a complex academic subject through the lens of poetry, and to be able to unpack and convey that to first, a cast of actors and second, an audience. Poetry takes time. The writer has to understand a subject in metaphorical terms to be able to capture it poetically. The multigenre approach makes it clear what aspects of the topic you do not yet grasp. It also opens the door to amazing discoveries.

Writing On Actors, Not For Actors

Playwriting is typically done by a playwright before the fact and given to actors and a director to bring to life through their different artistic sensibility. They are related but different disciplines. The playwright and the dramaturg on a production have more in common (in most cases – there are exceptions) than does the playwright with the director and cast.

Acting is a different way of knowing. Writing is both macrocosmic and microcosmic, while acting tends to be more particular to both the character and the actor playing the role. As with the folded paper exercise previously described, actors and writers provide different pieces of the puzzle, working together to make a whole.

However, there is a playwriting technique in which one actually develops the material collaboratively with the cast. This almost always involves improvisation. Playwright Karen Zacarías has developed plays in which she familiarizes actors with their characters and then asks them the questions she has about those characters. The same actors may then improvise scene work, which Zacarías goes on to develop independently and bring to a future rehearsal for a more refined level of exchange.

I wrote a play with students once in which we listed the events that had to happen for the plot to advance as we had already determined, then in small groups they play-acted those scenes as I circulated the room, recording the results. It is an interesting proposition in a group writing session to not have the roles cast – to allow different students to assume the same role. The result is a rich, complex character created by several people equally invested in who that person is and what drives that character's behavior. It is a fascinating process.

With *Fractals*, we began rehearsals with a draft that had already been through some revision, but that was open to more change as the text was set on our cast members, and as we experimented with movement, meaning, and the impact of delivering material chorally and individually.

Revision

Many students confuse revision and editing. I teach editing as being more to do with correctness, organization, and clarity. Revision is an effort to align the purpose of the writing with its voice and audience. It is an opportunity to determine the extent to which the writer's intentions are clearly conveyed – or not. It invites creative approaches to explore and express the content.

The biggest challenges in the revision of *Fractals* were in reconciling the distance between the way I heard the language in my mind and the way it actually sounded aloud. There were passages that were redundant. There were concepts that were unclear; and if they were unclear to the cast after multiple readings, certainly they would be to an audience on a single one. The single most demanding aspect of the piece was the strict 50-minute time limit as dictated by the Fringe Festival agreement. It provided an excellent lesson to me in economy of language, and in choosing only that which is essential in the piece to remain.

Multigenre writing

Whole books are devoted to this topic, whole articles, whole workshops. If you are unfamiliar, this is a work written by a single author that uses multiple genres to tell a story or communicate the subject matter of a subject – fiction or non-fiction. In teaching terms, multigenre writing can be used as an exploration of genre (most people are comfortable in one or two, but more requires a stretch creatively) and can be used as an assessment. It certainly reflects mastery of creative writing, if that is what one is evaluating. It demonstrates a deep understanding of a research topic or academic subject, if that is the knowledge being assessed. The best way to learn multigenre writing is to read works that use the technique – and to be willing to get out of the way and try some new styles of writing, thinking, creating, and communicating.

Tom Romano has written many books on the topic of multigenre writing itself as well as the teaching of it. For published models, the most accessible in my view include Michael Ondaatje's *The Collected Works of Billy the Kid*, and Nick Bantock's *Griffin and Sabine* trilogy. Bantock's work is often classified as an epistolary novel, but I find that it goes beyond that because of his inclusion of artwork and design in each of the documents he devises.

Many contemporary writers have included news articles, letters, and recipes in their narratives – and shifts in the points of view of a range of characters – but creating a work composed entirely of multigenre writing is a different proposition. Often there is a repetend, a creative device that repeats throughout the work and serves as a through-line to bridge transitions between pieces and unify the whole.

No matter the strategy, this need must be met – the work must be held together by more than its content. *Fractals* used both poetry and prose to explore its content for meaning, married spoken text to movement, and to a slight degree incorporated ASL. A future iteration of it would layer much more movement and ASL on the cast and ask actors to dance and dancers to act to a much greater degree.

EDUCATION

I have been working in education since 1992 and in that time have seen the benefit of incorporating the arts across the curriculum first-hand. My dissertation research involved the use of a theater technique to foster cross-cultural communication. I used plays and playwriting with elementary students to teach the science and social studies content for their standardized exams in a lasting and meaningful way. Even as an arts educator, there are opportunities to use one discipline to enrich the development of another. I have brought dance educators to music classrooms, and professional actors to work side by side with students both in the classroom and onstage.

Academic content means something different when explored through the arts. Arts education is enriched by the exploration of multiple artistic disciplines; of seeing what they say about one another, calling on different parts of the brain, discovering new voices and new perspectives. Many educators balk at this. They feel that if they personally don't know how to act, sing, dance, write plays, or make films that they cannot use these techniques in their classrooms.

I have observed for more than 25 years that students don't balk. They run with the opportunity. They see it as play, and as a means of expression. What enables the work to happen is to establish a learning environment where taking risks, trying new things, and making mistakes is the norm. Offering choices is also critical. These choices include the type of artistic expression a student prefers to use on a given project, and whether that student prefers to work alone or collaboratively.

The National Science Foundation introduced the acronym STEM (science, technology, engineering, math) in 2001. The original intention was to teach those disciplines in an integrated way to promote greater learning, engagement, and advancement from schooling into fields that require that knowledge and skill set. Critical-analytical thinking and problem-solving are intrinsic to this curricular approach.

There is no consensus on when the acronym STEAM was introduced, an acknowledgement of the crucial role the arts play in brain development and cultivating the creativity necessary for innovation. Suffice to say that some argue the merits of STEM v. STEAM, while others view it as an evolution in academic practice. I subscribe to the latter, that it is an evolution in practice – and I have, in fact, seen skilled educators use the arts to stimulate creativity and exercise problem-solving ability long before the acronym's existence. It is simply good pedagogy.

Richard Florida originally published *The Rise of the Creative Class* in 2002 and has released a revision enhanced by a decade of new research. In it he identifies the significance of creativity in people's work lives, irrespective of their profession or industry, and the emergence of a class of people unified by their engagement in creative work. He maintains that all people are creative, and he applies creativity to fields as diverse as urban studies, public policy, and economics: "I define the core of the Creative Class to include people in science and engineering, architecture and design, education, arts, music, and entertainment whose economic function is to create new ideas, new technology, and new creative content."

Florida articulates the need to apply creativity across the spectrum of the world of work. "The only way forward is to make all jobs creative jobs, infusing service work, manufacturing work, farming, and every other form of human endeavor with creativity and human potential." The only way to begin to accomplish this is by integrating creativity and academics in the classroom in ways that permeate the curriculum.

Maryam Mirzakhani (1977-2017) was the first woman to win the Fields Medal, the most prestigious award in mathematics. Her earliest dreams were of becoming a writer, and math was her weakest academic subject. She came to see the poetry in math, which broke open her understanding of it.

By the time she left high school, she won a gold medal in the 1995 International Mathematical Olympiad with a perfect score. Her students recall her use of drawing to work through complex mathematical problems. "It's almost like she had a window on the math landscape, and she was trying to describe how the things living there interacted with each other," said student Jenya Sapir.

Mirzakhani sketched and doodled her way through new ideas, abstractions, dimensions different from our own, and then translated those into the language of mathematics. She claimed that the process of drawing helped her to forge connections. In her brief lifetime, she contributed advancements in Teichmüller theory, hyperbolic geometry, ergodic theory, and symplectic geometry – through the use of drawing and an understanding of mathematics as poetry.

Josh Jones reports in a 2017 Open Culture piece that John Coltrane made a drawing of a tone circle that scholars have connected to both physics and geometry. He quotes blogger and musician Roel Hollander: "Thelonius Monk once said, 'All musicians are subconsciously mathematicians.' Musicians like John Coltrane have been very much aware of the mathematics of music and consciously applied it to his works."

The concept of the circle of fifths is based on the work of Pythagoras, as far back as 600 B.C.E. By experimenting with different lengths of vibrating string, he discovered relationships among the pitches. He defined the octave and divided it into half pitches. This is the foundation for Coltrane's tone circle and a whole school of thought known as sonic geometry.

Cosmologist, theoretical physicist, and saxophone player Stephon Alexander speaks to the intersection of science, mathematics and music throughout his work, notably in his 2016 book, *The Jazz of Physics*. He recognizes Einstein's inspiration of Coltrane, and the deliberate physics and geometry at the core of Coltrane's music. He explores the concept of the Music of the Spheres (also explored in *Fractals*) as intrinsic to the interconnected workings of the cosmos at its most fundamental. He believes in keeping things simple, of stripping the most sophisticated scientific ideas to their greatest simplicity, and that often the physical world is best understood through its musical expression.

The world is interconnected in all of its aspects, yet we endeavor to tease it apart in the classroom and teach its component parts in isolation. This approach has never made sense to me. Coltrane's tone circle is a perfect example of how the universe can be understood at

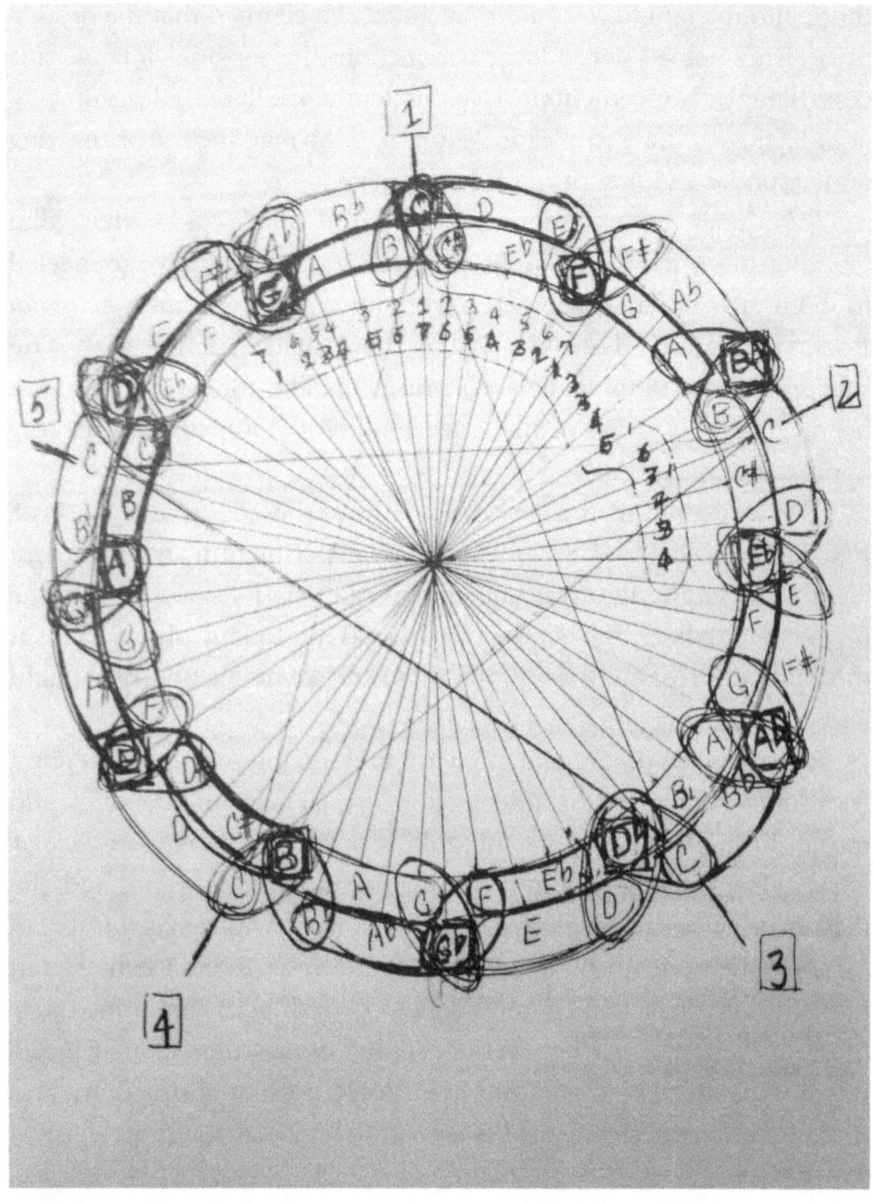

Tone circles are a geometric expression of the 12 pitch classes, the most familiar of which is the Circle of 4ths and 5ths. Coltrane's variation of the Circle of 4ths and 5ths is constructed in such a way that a pentagram and a pentagon appear when a straight line is drawn between the same tones.

the intersection of its characteristics – in this case, music, geometry, and physics – rather than by their separation.

These are but a few of the stories of people using arts and academics interchangeably to advance the value of each, of both. These stories are happening all around us, every day.

Judith Lynne Hanna's 2015 work, *Dancing to Learn: The Brain's Cognition, Emotion and Movement* is often hailed as a must-read for dance educators, but it contains myriad applications for educational settings outside of the arts. She presents dance as "a serious mode of inquiry and discovery" and makes a case for movement as the neuronal basis for associative learning, consolidation of memory, even the generation of new brain cells and connections – the ability to grow in our intellect over a lifetime rather than lose mental capacity as we age.

Hanna explains the development of neural mirroring through movement and dance that enables us to better identify the feelings and mental states of those around us, increasing our capacity for cooperation and empathy. She cites research showing the neuroplasticity of the brain and the gains in cognition, attention, sensory-motor performance, memory, and a number of other areas after only six months of dance instruction.

Because dance is a language system, similar to poetry, ongoing exposure to dance increases language ability including the use of metaphor, abstraction, verbal language, and syntax processing. She profiles a number of schools and outreach programs that have embedded dance in their curricula, and reports the significant improvements in language acquisition, memory, and confidence those students experience. She describes the reciprocal relationship between thought and movement, "The way we think influences the way we speak and move, but the influence also goes the other way."

We can work from the outside in; we can change the way we think by changing the way we move, alone and in relationship to others. Hanna's interest ranges from the way a person performs and perceives dance to the way that person learns other domains of knowledge through dance. Her compelling and well-documented body of research insists that we make deliberate connections between movement and learning.

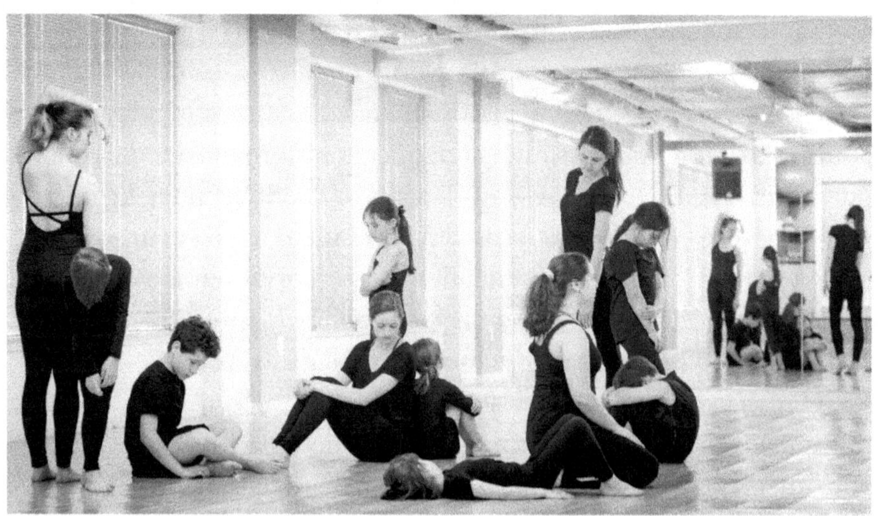

Groundshare Arts Alliance in rehearsal
Photo credit: D. Ohlandt

Amanda Whiteman, our text choreographer for *Fractals*, incorporates these concepts into her work on a regular basis. She is the founder and director of Groundshare Arts Alliance:

A collection of teaching artists, performers and arts integration educators working to bring collaborative performing arts experiences to the community. Through classes, workshops, performances and residencies our professional artists work alongside students to create and explore the artistic process together. (groundsharearts.com)

I asked her about her summer *Dirt and Dance* camps, through which she teaches both dance and the science of the natural world. She identifies her primary goals as giving children a way to deepen their observation skills, helping them learn to sit and be quiet for short periods as they observe and experience the natural world, and making connections between the natural world and movement, which they create daily after returning from a natural setting to the studio.

She also mentioned the experience her daughter, then five years old, had the summer we created and performed *Fractals*, noteworthy because it is so closely in keeping with Hanna's findings in *Dancing to Learn*. Whiteman told me that her daughter was still talking about it a year later, that it opened her eyes and gave her a new way to see the world. She was able to organize her world with new perspective, and it gave her new language with which to convey this. If this is the lasting impact that a 50-minute piece of theater can have on a five-year-old, there is no limit to the ways this can be applied in the classroom regardless of whether arts or academics are the focus of instruction.

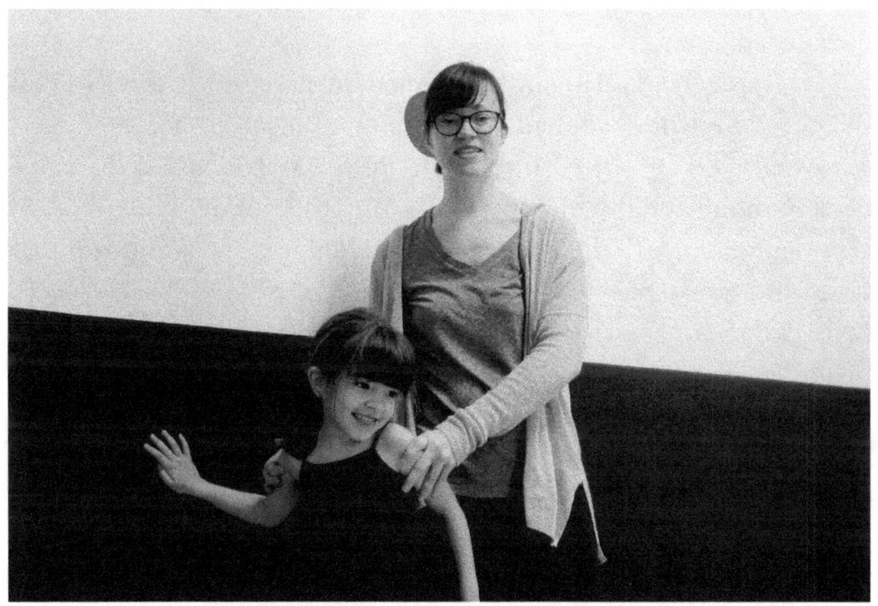

Amanda Whiteman and her daughter,
a member of Groundshare Arts Alliance
Photo credit: Kate O'Toole

A New York City-based nonprofit, STEM From Dance, has received a lot of attention in recent years for its use of dance toward several ends: to develop confidence in young women through dance; to help them make connections between dance and academics; and ultimately to lead them to learn engineering, coding, and computer science. They apply their evolving technological proficiency toward designing their dance performances and transfer their confidence in themselves as dancers to the belief that they can thrive in fields that have not typically been accessible to women, particularly women of color. The program offers an encouraging model for using the arts and academics, in school settings, camps, and workshops, to foster greater facility in both domains.

The poet Stanley Burnshaw famously wrote, "Poetry begins with the body and ends with the body." The performance of *Fractals* is comprised of the poetry of dance and of the spoken word and can serve as a model and springboard for classroom applications across the curriculum.

Educator Karla Hogan mentioned in a recent interview that she wondered how students might communicate other literature, *Macbeth*, or *Lord of the Flies*, through dance? We discussed the value of communicating without words, of discovering metaphorical representations of the rich ideas embedded in literature that transcend story. She used the example of Alvin Ailey's *Revelation*, saying that you can see what the words mean, you can see the meanings of words such as slavery and freedom. This strategy, to encounter the human experience both individually and universally, and to engage it in depth, invites the regular use of movement and dance in academic classrooms.

In addition to deepening literature study, *Fractals* is a model of how to learn, explore, research, and express the complex worlds of fractal geometry, nature, art, architecture, biology, medicine, finance, philosophy, religion and spirituality, through poetry and dance.

In a March 2018 op-ed piece for *The Washington Post*, mathematician Satyan Linus Devadoss says that upon learning his profession, strangers often remark that he must be smart. He posits the following "spectrum of smart" in our culture: art < literature < history < economics < biology < math. He also points out its flaw, that it misunderstands the differences between measurability and complexity. "Although measurability increases toward the right of the spectrum, complexity increases toward the left."

Math and science are "less messy, yielding more accurate solutions, whereas ideas in the humanities are more complicated, resulting in less precision." He also suggests that the questions raised by the humanities are the more difficult and ultimately, more difficult to solve:

Complexity is inversely related to measurability. Scientific marvels surround us: splitting atoms, peering into black holes and manipulating genomes. Yet the 21st century continues to grapple with the basic themes and issues encountered in the humanities over the centuries: gender and race, beauty and acceptance, truth and power . . . These problems are not rocket science, they are far more difficult than rocket science. Putting a man on the moon is the easy stuff.

He concludes that "science is about the simple 'could,' not the complex 'should.'"

Collaborating across artistic disciplines, examining academic worlds through the lens of the arts, seeing and expressing our world view through multiple genres, these all give us the means to engage in complexity, to live at the intersection of both "could" and "should." They enable us to experience a world that is interconnected in its greatest and smallest aspects, and to communicate that understanding to others, the content of our understanding driving the form by which it is conveyed. They allow us to begin a conversation that grows as other voices join in, a common language with countless dialects, discovering one another and the world we inhabit through a collaborative engagement with the arts.

ACKNOWLEDGEMENTS

The following people and organizations were instrumental to the writing, research, and completion of this book:

Meredith Barnes and DanceArtTheater

Greg Butler

Paula Leggett Chase

Liz Colandene

Tomé Cousin

Shu-Chen Cuff

Rick Davis

Marcel Artes Deolazo

Autumn Eckman

Jack Ferver

Patricia Foreman

Echo Montgomery Garrett and Lucid House Publishing

Karla Hogan

Ruth Judson

LeeAnn Altman Kole

Theo Kossenas and Media4Artists

Jessi Shull

Tom Teasley

Chao Tian

Bartholomäus Traubeck

Constance Walsh

Amanda Whiteman

Workhouse Arts Center

Karen Zacarías

RESOURCES

These are works that may have been mentioned in the text of this book or may have informed my understanding of the subject matter. I provide them with brief explanation here to help the reader pursue those sources of greatest benefit to a range of purposes and interests.

CHILDREN

Theo Buchanan; *Power of Patterns: Fractals* (Time for Kids Non-Fiction Readers, 2017)

> Upper elementary and middle school readers. Excellent overview of the subject with attention to Euclidian and fractal geometry, fractals and nature, fractals and the human body, Mandelbrot and Julia sets.

Sarah C. Campbell; *Mysterious Patterns: Finding Fractals in Nature* (Boyds Mills Press, 2014

> Grade 2 and up. Includes information on Euclidian and fractal geometry, Mandelbrot, self-similarity, branching patterns. Make Your Own Fractal activity.

Creative Haven; *Nature Fractals Coloring Book* (Dover Publications, Inc., 2014)

> Grade 6 and up. Fractal patterns found in nature with brief explanation.

Theoni Pappas; *Fractals, Googols and Other Mathematical Tales* (Wide World Publishing, 1993)

> Grade 2 and up. Range of math topics. Information and activities. Includes Fibonacci sequence, fractals, golden mean.

Julien Clinton Sprott; *Fractals Coloring Book* (Chartwell Books, 2014)

> All ages. Range of fractal shapes and patterns varying in complexity. Some are simple enough for early childhood and primary grades. Overview of subject precedes coloring pages.

FRACTALS

BOOKS

Kenneth Falconer; *Fractals: A Very Short Introduction* (Oxford University Press, 2013)

> Fractal geometry, fractals in art and in the natural world. Explanations are detailed and in mathematical terms.

Michael Frame and Amelia Urry; *Fractal Worlds: Grown, Built, and Imagined* (Yale University Press, 2016)

> Distillation of Frame's Yale University course on Fractal Geometry. Co-written by poet Amelia Urry. Fractals in nature, art, medicine, and technology. Complex mathematical instruction made accessible to general public by way of Urry's prose explanations.

Doug Harrington; *Fractal Art: A Coloring Book* (Pomegranate Communications, Inc., 2016)

> Adult coloring book. Shapes are complex and require skilled fine motor function.

Benoit B. Mandelbrot; *The Fractal Geometry of Nature* (W.H. Freeman and Company, 1977)

The Fractal Bible. Mandelbrot's expression of his discovery in mathematical terms. Comprehensive overview of the phenomenon and the field in all its aspects. Prose passages are accessible, mathematics is complex.

Manfred Schroeder; *Fractals, Chaos, Power Laws: Minutes from an Infinite Paradise* (Dover Publications, Inc., 1991)

Introduction provides a helpful overview accessible to the general reader. Detailed examinations of self-similarity, noise and sound wave patterns, Cantor sets, Fibonacci sequencing, practical applications of fractals to stock market analysis, gambling, crowd behavior, structures in outer space, cellular growth and decay, among others.

INTRODUCING…SERIES (Icon Books, Ltd.)

Series of graphic guides which make complex subjects accessible to the general reader. Each is an overview of its subject matter and provides both good working knowledge of the subject matter and direction for further inquiry.

Highly recommended for work with students as a model of work that they themselves go on to produce to exhibit mastery of a subject.

Nigel Lesmoir-Gordon, Will Rood & Ralph Edney;l *Introducing Fractals: A Graphic Guide* (2013)

J.P. McEvoy & Oscar Zarate; *Introducing Quantum Theory: A Graphic Guide* (2013)

Ziauddin Sardar & Iwona Abrams; *Introducing Chaos: A Graphic Guide* (2013)

DVD

Michael Schwarz & Bill Jersey; *Fractals: Hunting the Hidden Dimension* (NOVA for PBS Home Video, 2008)

> Best possible resource for educational overview of fractals. Visual information provides clarity and engages interest. Content includes explanation, history, and applications to fashion, film, medicine, technology, and the environment, among others. Highly recommended for general knowledge, upper elementary to adult. Isolated segments could be used with younger learners. Corresponding website contains lesson plans and classroom activities for grades 6-8 and 9-12.
>
> https://www.pbs.org/wgbh/nova/physics/hunting-hidden-dimension.html
>
> Classroom guide:
>
> https://www.pbs.org/wgbh/nova/teachers/programs/3514_fractals.html
>
> Classroom activities:
>
> https://www.pbs.org/wgbh/nova/teachers/activities/3514_fractals.html

RELATED AREAS OF STUDY

Silvia Bigliazzi & Sharon Wood, eds.; *Collaboration in the Arts from the Middle Ages to the Present* (Routledge, 2017)

> Collection of interdisciplinary scholarly essays on artistic collaboration between artists whether they are contemporaries or building on one another's work across time. Several of the key concepts are mentioned in the Introduction to this book.

Leonard da Vinci, translated by Jean Paul; Richter,1888; *The Notebooks of Leonardo da Vinci, Complete & Illustrated* (e-Kitap Projesi & Cheapest Books, 2014)

Pertinent to this work are his notes on Vitruvian Man and the Golden Ratio.

Richard Florida; *The Rise of the Creative Class, Revisited* (Basic Books, 2011)

Examination of the role of creativity in our lives, requiring that we change the way that creativity is valued and the way we cultivate it in ourselves and in one another. Among Florida's detailed discussions are the ways that creativity impacts the economy, our work, our individual lives, and our communities.

DANCE

Martha Graham; *The Notebooks of Martha Graham.* (Harcourt Brace Jovanovich, Inc., 1973)

Excellent model for thinking about choreography/dance from multiple vantage points and devising notation to capture them. Movement is noted alongside ideas, quotations, conceptual underpinnings of pieces.

Judith Lynne Hanna; *Dancing to Learn: The Brain's Cognition, Emotion, and Movement.* (Rowman & Littlefield, 2015)

Critically important text for educators across all disciplines. Empirical data, research, and anecdotal accounts of the interactions among brain development, movement/dance, and academic learning.

Katherine Teck; *Ear Training for the Body: A Dancer's Guide to Music.* (Princeton Book Co., 1994)

Musical training for dancers. Includes musicality, body percussion, choreography as collaboration, and a movement-oriented approach to the fundamentals of music.

MUSIC

Stephon Alexander; *The Jazz of Physics: The Secret Link Between Music and the Structure of the Universe.* (Basic Books, 2016)

> Uses the Coltrane tone circle as the jumping-off place for an exploration of the intersection of jazz, geometry, spirituality, and physics. Pertinent to the study of fractals are sections addressing Pythagoras, Music of the Spheres, and the interconnectedness of the natural world. Alexander is a frequent speaker on the subject and understands the subject matter deeply, as a saxophonist, a theoretical physicist, and cosmologist.

> Recommended: The Jazz of Physics, Stephon Alexander, TEDxSanDiego

> https://www.youtube.com/watch?v=v9_ZzY99-6U

MUSICAL THEATER

Peter Filichia; *Broadway Musicals: The Biggest Hit & The Biggest Flop of the Season 1959-2009.* (Applause Theater & Cinema Books, 2010)

> Detailed reference used extensively in Chapter 5 of this book to analyze the relationship between theater and dance where dance is used to extend and continue storytelling and make an artistic statement beyond its entertainment value.

Larry Stempel; *Showtime: A History of the Broadway Musical Theater.* (W. W. Norton & Co., Inc., 2010)

> Comprehensive musical theater history, 1849-2008. Exhaustively researched. Colored plates, photographs, and print music excerpts clarify and expand the information conveyed through organized and accessible prose.

NOTES

INTRODUCTION

'Collaboration in the Arts from the Middle Ages to the Present,' ed. Silvia Bigliazzi and Sharon Wood (2006; New York, New York; Routledge) 1, 7, 34-35, 53, 79-80, 85,177-178.

CHAPTER 1: ORIGINS

"the science of surprises":
https://fractalfoundation.org/resources/what-is-chaos-theory/

definition:
https://fractalfoundation.org/resources/what-are-fractals/#:~:text=Fractals%20are%20infinitely%20complex%20patterns,systems%20%E2%80%93%20the%20pictures%20of%20Chaos.

Fractal images from plot points on graph:
https://fractaltodesktop.com/mandelbrot-set-basics/index.html

Cancer research, global warming, CGI;
James Brown, University of New Mexico, "invisible world made visible":
Fractals: Hunting the Hidden Dimension (2009; Boston, WGBH Educational Foundation) DVD

"Worship as many as you see and more will appear!":
Shaffer, Peter, *Equus.* (1974; New York, Samuel French Ltd.) 53.

Bartholomäus Traubeck:
http://traubeck.com/works/years

CHAPTER 2: DEVELOPMENT

Amazed and Confused, Heather Zempel (2014; Nashville, Tennessee; Thomas Nelson) 25-29.

Bartholomäus Traubeck: http://traubeck.com/works/years

Personal interview, Meredith Barnes, 8-25-17.

Personal interview, Amanda Whiteman, 8-21-17.

Groundshare Arts Alliance: http://groundsharearts.com/

CHAPTER 3: THE TEXT

Much of the factual information provided in the annotated text can be found in Wikipedia unless otherwise noted below.

Vitruvian Man:
https://leonardodavinci.stanford.edu/submissions/clabaugh/history/leonardo.html
https://www.bl.uk/learning/cult/bodies/vitruvius/proportion.html

"From knee to foot, from elbow to fingertip One quarter of a person's height A golden ratio":
https://www.livescience.com/37704-phi-golden-ratio.html

"Evidence of a plan
Amid the chaos of being human":
Chaos theory and fractals
http://fractalfoundation.org/resources/what-is-chaos-theory/

"Pythagoras
Used the circle to represent the spiritual realm,
The square, the material world":
Architecture and Mathematics from Antiquity to the Future: Volume One: Antiquity to the 1500s, Kim Williams and Michael J. Ostwald (2015; Basel, Switzerland; Birkhäuser Verlag) 82-83.

The Influence of Mathematics on the Development of Structural Form, "Holger Falter. In *Nexus II: Architecture and Mathematics,* 'ed. Kim Williams. (1998; Florence, Italy; Edizioni dell'Erba) 51-64.

Enrico Giaccherini identifies this as a type of collaboration
Collaboration in the Arts from the Middle Ages to the Present, ed. Silvia Bigliazzi and Sharon Wood (2006; New York, New York; Routledge) Chapter 1.

"Studying population
Multiplying rabbits
Finding a solution In a sequence of numbers":
Fractals, Chaos, Power Laws: Minutes from an Infinite Paradise, Manfred Schroeder (2009; New York, New York; W.H. Freeman and Company) Ch. 5, 13.

Koch curve, Mandelbrot and the English coastline, Cohen antenna, branching patterns and the rainforest:
The Fractal Geometry of Nature, Benoit Mandelbrot (1975; New York, New York; W. H. Freeman and Company)

James Brown, University of New Mexico, "invisible world made visible":
Fractals: Hunting the Hidden Dimension (2009; Boston, WGBH Educational Foundation) DVD

"Benoit Mandelbrot
Realizing the work
Of Julia and Fatou…":
Fractal Worlds: Grown, Built, and Imagined, Michael Frame and Amelia
Urry (2016; New Haven, Connecticut; Yale University Press)

"She raises an umbrella
No response
She waits for rescue":
Amazed and Confused, Heather Zempel (2014; Nashville, Tennessee;
Thomas Nelson) 25-29.

"Fractals
Their logic, design
Attraction
Is their power":
Fractals, A Graphic Guide, Nigel Lesmoir-Gordon, Will Rood and Ralph
Edney (2013; London, England; Icon Books Ltd.)

"They provide
Order, sense
Safety
In a world that looks
On its surface
Tumultuous, disordered":
https://fractalfoundation.org/resources/what-is-chaos-theory/

"Pollock understood
Layering paint
Imitating nature
Adopting its dynamics":
http://discovermagazine.com/2001/nov/featpollock

'Van Gogh captured
The patterns in the turbulence
Rather than the
Darkness of the night":
mic.com
https://mic.com/articles/104354/van-gogh-s-paintings-accurately-depict-one-of-our-most-complex-scientific-theories#.wfRUBX286
nature.com
https://www.nature.com/news/2006/060703/full/news060703-17.html
TED-Ed
https://ed.ted.com/lessons/the-unexpected-math-behind-van-gogh-s-starry-night-natalya-st-clair

"Hokusai saw
The crest of the wave
Not its danger
The wings of a bird
Not its distance":
https://users.math.yale.edu/public_html/People/frame/Fractals/Panorama/Art/Hokusai/Hokusai.html

Mandelbrot and the English coastline
https://science.sciencemag.org/content/156/3775/636

Richardson, Mandelbrot, coastline paradox
https://mathsection.com/from-coastlines-to-fractals/?cookie-state-change=1594486824114

"A cluster of trees
Predicting the pattern
Of the forest
Exhaling the oxygen
We take into lungs
That bear their shape
Carried away by a network
Of self-same branching
Vessels":
A reference to West, Brown and Enquist's work on C02 emissions in the rain forest:
Fractals: Hunting the Hidden Dimension(2009; Boston, WGBH Educational Foundation) DVD

"We tame the chaos of motion
Into the rhythms of dance
The twos and fours
Of our heartbeats
The rhythms of Euclid"
A reference to Catherine Turocy's work on Baroque dance and fractals
https://www.academia.edu/9472878/Baroque_Dance_and_fractals
Also, use of branching pattern (fractal) of circulatory system to diagnose heart failure
https://www.ncbi.nlm.nih.gov/pubmed/8678358

Bartholomäus Traubeck:
http://traubeck.com/works/years
See also
http://www.cpr.org/classical/blog/turntable-plays-tree-rings-instead-vinyl-grooves-how-did-he-do
Interviews
https://www.datagarden.org/blog/bartholomaus-traubeck-on-years
https://www.huffingtonpost.com/2012/02/01/huffpost-arts-interviews-_n_1247581.html

YouTube recording of 'Years'
https://www.youtube.com/watch?v=12dc4IQGnFc]

The Prince of Tides, Pat Conroy (1986; Boston, Massachusetts; Houghton Mifflin Company) 566.

CHAPTER 5: APPLICATIONS

Show listings and descriptions based on personal experience and/or information as provided by Wikipedia

Dance Theater
Personal interview, Tomé Cousin, 9-12-20.
The Total Theater Artist and New Media Performance, Tomé Cousin. Master's thesis. (2008; Lambert Academic Publishing)
Kant, Marion. "Oscar Schlemmer's *Triadic Ballet* (Paris, 1932) and Dance Discourse in Germany. Three Letters with Annotation and a Commentary."
Dance Research: The Journal of the Society for Dance Research 33, no. 1 (2015): 16-30.
Kurt Jooss
https://www.dance-teacher.com/kurt-jooss-2392328615.html
Tanztheater and Pina Bausch
https://www.nytimes.com/2020/01/15/arts/dance/pina-bausch-bluebeard-revival.html

Synetic Theater
https://synetictheater.org/

Rotimi Agbabiaka for Theater Bay Area Online: https://www.theatrebayarea.org/news/189872/The-Rise-of-Dance-Theatre.htm

Dance Theater, Kellundra Smith, American Theater Online
https://www.americantheatre.org/2016/02/23/dance-or-theatre-yes/

What Acting Skills Do You Want to See in Your Dancers?, Simi Horwitz. https://www.backstage.com/magazine/article/acting-skills-want-see-dancers-63272/

Bill T. Jones
https://newyorklivearts.org/btj-az-company/currently-touring/

Showtime: A History of the Broadway Musical Theater, Larry Stempel (2010; New York, New York; W. W. Norton and Company, Inc.) 569

The Stanislavski System: The Professional Training of an Actor, Sonia Moore (1960; New York, New York; Penguin Books)

Personal interview, Constance Walsh, 10-18-17.

The Notebooks of Martha Graham, Martha Graham (1973; New York, New York; Harcourt Brace Jovanovich)

Personal interview, Autumn Eckman, 10-10-17 and 6-8-20.

Personal interview, Jessi Shull, 10-10-17.

Personal interview, Tomé Cousin, 9-12-20.

Tomé Cousin bio and term "interdisciplinary artist"
https://www.drama.cmu.edu/people/faculty-staff/tomecousin/

The Total Theater Artist and New Media Performance, Tomé Cousin. Master's thesis. (2008; Lambert Academic Publishing)

Review, *Through the Wall*, Capital Fringe Festival 2018
https://www.washingtonpost.com/news/arts-and-entertainment/wp/2018/07/20/elan-zafirs-personal-the-unaccompanied-minor-is-a-top-pick-this-week-at-the-fringe-festival/

Marcel Artes Deolazo
https://thehornypotter.com/about-me/
https://thehornypotter.bigcartel.com/

Collaboration in the Arts from the Middle Ages to the Present, ed. Silvia Bigliazzi and Sharon Wood (2006; New York, New York; Routledge) 1, 7, 34-35, 53, 79-80, 85,177-178.

Personal interview, Tomé Cousin, 9-12-20.

Body Painting (Tseng Kwong Chi, Keith Harin, Bill T. Jones) http://www.kasmingallery.com/exhibitions/2010-02-11_tseng-kwong-chi

Goldman, Danielle. "Ghostcatching: An intersection of Technology, Labor, and Race." *Dance Research Journal* 35, no. 2 – 36, no. 1 (2003-2004): 68-87.

Blending Genre, Altering Style, Tom Romano (2000; Portsmouth, New Hampshire; Heinemann)

The Collected Works of Billy the Kid, Michael Ondaatje (1996; New York, New York; Vintage)

The Griffin and Sabine Trilogy, Nick Bantock (1991; San Francisco, California; Chronicle Books)

National Science Foundation and STEM education
https://www.nsf.gov/

The Rise of the Creative Class, Richard Florida (2011; New York, New York; Basic Books) xiv, 8.

Maryam Mirzakhani
https://www.nytimes.com/interactive/2017/12/28/magazine/the-lives-they-lived-maryam-mirzakhani.html

Coltrane tone circle
https://roelhollander.eu/en/blog-saxophone/coltrane-tone-circle/

The Jazz of Physics, Stephon Alexander. (2016; New York, New York; Basic Books)
3-5, 222-223.
Stephon Alexander interview, PBS/Nova Science Now
https://www.pbs.org/video/secret-life-of-scientists-stephon-alexander-theoretical-physicist/
Stephon Alexander, TEDx San Diego 2015
https://www.youtube.com/watch?v=v9_ZzY99-6U

Dancing To Learn: The Brain's Cognition, Emotion and Movement, Judith Lynne Hanna. (2014; Lanham, Maryland; Rowman and Littlefield)

Groundshare Arts Alliance
http://groundsharearts.com/

STEM from Dance:
https://www.stemfromdance.org/articles/2020/2/18/new-york-city-teens-are-learning-coding-and-science-through-dance

https://www.forbes.com/sites/evaamsen/2020/02/15/new-york-city-teens-are-learning-coding-and-science-through-dance/#6d5519712bba

https://www.dancemagazine.com/stem-dance-2584325613.html

Personal interview, Karla Hogan, 3-16-18.

A Math Problem for Pi Day, Satyan Linus Devadoss.
https://www.washingtonpost.com/opinions/a-math-problem-for-pi-day/2018/03/14/7d562a78-27be-11e8-bc72-077aa4dab9ef_story.html

ABOUT THE AUTHOR

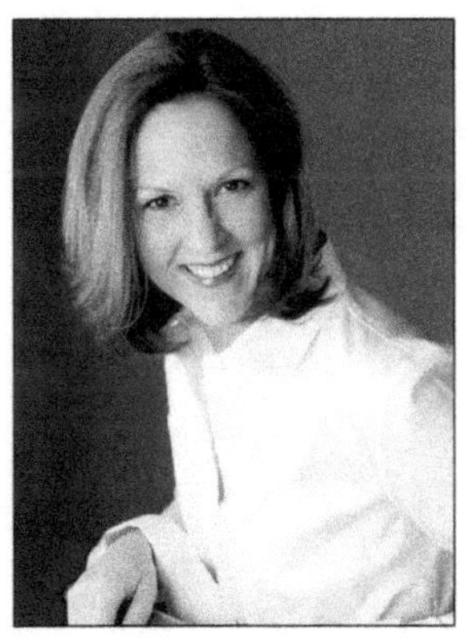

Kimberley Cetron

Kimberley **Cetron** began her career in professional theater as an actor, singer, dancer, and pianist. From there she expanded into producing, directing, music directing, costume design, choreography, and dramaturgy. She began her teaching career through music education, completing a Master's degree in Early Childhood and Elementary Education and teaching multiple academic subjects at every level from pre-kindergarten through graduate school.

During her doctoral work in education, an advisor asked why she had separated her performance and education experiences and urged her to combine them. Her dissertation research was a qualitative, longitudinal study of fostering cross-cultural communication using theater techniques. Her previous writing has included poetry, educational journals, book reviews, and playwriting. She has done staff development and curriculum writing for the Fairfax County Public Schools and taught undergraduate theater and graduate education at George Mason University. She lives in Virginia with her husband, Adam, and her son, Gabriel.

INDEX